you
and **your toddler**

other titles in the You and Your Child Series
Editor, Dr A. H. Brafman

you and your baby: a baby's emotional life
   Frances Thomson Salo
you and your child: making sense of learning disabilities
   Sheila and Martin Hollins

ORDERS
tel: +44 (0)20 8969 4454; fax: +44 (0)20 8969 5585
email: shop@karnacbooks.com
www.karnacbooks.com

you
and **your toddler**

Jenny Stoker

You and Your Child Series
Editor, Dr A. H. Brafman

KARNAC

LONDON   NEW YORK

First published in 2005 by
H. Karnac (Books) Ltd.
6 Pembroke Buildings, London NW10 6RE

Copyright © 2005 Jenny Stoker

British Library Cataloguing in Publication Data

A C.I.P. for this book is available from the British Library

ISBN: 1-85575-368-5

10 9 8 7 6 5 4 3 2 1

Edited, designed, and produced by Communication Crafts

Printed in Great Britain

www.karnacbooks.com

to Kate, Robert, and Jess

contents

about the author

Jenny Stoker, a psychoanalyst who works with adults and children, is also a member of staff at the Anna Freud Centre and has run a parent–toddler group there for many years. In the past she has worked for the NHS in an outpatient psychotherapy department. She contributes both to academic journals and to magazines for parents and allied professionals. She teaches students at the Anna Freud Centre and has been a seminar leader for the series of introductory lectures at the Institute of Psychoanalysis.

acknowledgements

I would like to thank my editor, Dr Brafman, for his encouragement, advice, and faith in my capacity to produce this book. Thanks are due, too, to my colleagues Angela Joyce and Marie Zaphiriou Woods for their helpful comments. Thanks are also due to David Norgrove for his patience and clarity of thought as well as much else besides. I am also indebted to my assistants and the rest of the toddler team staff and students at the Anna Freud Centre. Finally, and most importantly, I am immensely grateful to all the toddlers and their parents with whom I have worked and from whom I have learned so much.

series editor's foreword

Dr A. H. BRAFMAN

Few birthdays are celebrated with such enthusiasm, pride, and happiness as a child's first. The helpless infant of twelve months earlier is now showing innumerable signs of his personality and engaging in interactions that bring powerful emotions to his parents and give them the feeling that all the struggles of caring for their baby have been well worth it. In this volume of our series of books on child development, Jenny Stoker portrays with warmth and sensitivity the unfolding of the second and third years of the baby's life, now promoted to toddlerhood, with its new developmental hurdles for the child and new challenges for the parents. Jenny describes and discusses these steps in a manner that should be very helpful to parents.

There is a central philosophy uniting all the volumes in the You and Your Child Series. Each of the authors featured has published papers and books for the academic and clinical communities; the present volumes, however, are specifically aimed at parents. The intent is not to convince but to inform the reader. Rather than offering solutions, we are describing, explaining, and discussing the problems that parents meet while bringing up their children, from infancy through to adulthood.

We envisage that two groups of parents may choose to read these books: some may wish to find here answers to specific questions or to problems they are facing in their lives, whereas others may read them only to broaden their knowledge of human development. Our intention is that the writing should be phrased in a way that might satisfy both groups. There is an attempt at something of a translation of what children of different ages experience in their lives with parents, family, and the wider world. Our authors have based their texts on their extensive work with children, adolescents, and their parents— not only in the authors' private consulting-rooms, but also in schools, community agencies, and teaching hospitals—and, in most cases, with children of their own.

The authors aim to depict the child's experiential view of his life, helping parents to understand behaviours, thoughts, and feelings that the child may not have been able to verbalize. There is no question of being the child's advocate—no purpose is seen in trying to find who is to blame for the problems under discussion. These are, rather, interested and knowledgeable professionals attempting to get child and parents to understand each other's point of view. In our books, the authors describe in detail the increasing range of each child's developing abilities on the path from infancy to adulthood: it is this knowledge of potential and actual abilities that is fundamental for an understanding of a child's behaviour.

Many, if not most, of the books available on child development adopt the view that a child is the product of the environment in which he is brought up. To some extent, this is obviously true: the child will speak his parents' language and adopt the customs that characterize the culture in which the family live. The commonly heard remark that a particular child "takes after" a parent or other close relation bears out the fact that each growing individual responds and adapts to the milieu in which he lives—and not only in childhood, but throughout his life. Nevertheless, it is still true that not all children brought up in one particular home will show the same characteristics. From a scientific point of view, there are endless discussions on the issue of nature versus nurture. However, from a pragmatic point of view, it is certainly more correct and more useful to consider family problems with children as being the result of an interaction—who started this, and when and how it started, is virtually impossible to establish. Through their words and be- haviour, child and parents continually confirm each other's expectations; they keep a vicious circle going, where each of them feels totally justified in their views of themselves and of each other.

It is not rare that the parents present quite different read- ings of what each of them considers their child's problems to be. Needless to say, the same can be found when considering any single issue in the life of an ordinary family. The baby cries: the mother thinks he is hungry, whereas the father may feel that here is an early warning of a child who will wish to control his parents' lives. The toddler refuses some particular food: the mother resents this early sign of rebellion, whereas the father will claim that the child is actually showing that he can discrimi- nate between pleasant and undesirable flavours. The 5-year-old demands a further hour of television watching: the mother agrees that he should share a programme she happens to enjoy, whereas the father explodes at the pointlessness of trying to instil a sense of discipline in the house. By the time the child has reached puberty or adolescence, these clashes are a matter of daily routine. . . . From a practical point of view, it is important to recognize that there is no question of ascertaining which parent is right or which one is wrong: within their personal frames of reference, they are both right. The problem with such disagreements is that, whatever happens, the child will always be agreeing with one of them and opposing the other.

There is no doubt that each parent forms an individual interpretation of the child's behaviour in line with his or her own upbringing and personality, view of him/herself in the world, and past and present experiences, some of them conscious and most of them unconscious. But—what about the child in question? It is not part of ordinary family life that a child should be asked for *his* explanation of the behaviour that has led to the situation where the parents disagree on its interpretation. Unfortunately, if he is asked, it can happen that he fails to find the words to explain himself, or occasionally he is driven to say what he believes the parent wants to hear, or at other times his words sound too illogical to be believed. The myth has somehow grown that in such circumstances only a professional will have the capacity to fathom out the child's "real" motives and intentions.

It is an obvious fact that each family will have its own style of approaching its child. It is simply unavoidable that each individual child will have his development influenced—not *determined* but *affected*—by the responses his behaviour brings out in his parents. It is, however, quite difficult for parents to appreciate the precise developmental abilities achieved by their child. No child can operate, cope with life, or respond to stimuli beyond his particular abilities at any particular point in time. And this is *the* point addressed in the present series of books. We try to provide portraits of the various stages in the child's cognitive, intellectual, and emotional development and how these unfolding stages affect not only the child's experience of himself, but also how he perceives and relates to the world in which he lives. Our hope is that establishing this context will help the parents who read these books to see their child from a different perspective.

A note on the use of pronouns

In general discussions in this Series, for simplicity of language, masculine pronouns are used to denote the child and feminine pronouns the parent. Unless specified by the context, the word "parent" should be taken to mean mother, father, or other significant caregiver.

you
and your toddler

introduction

Most parents will greet their child's first birthday with pleasure and a sense of achievement. Their child has made huge visible progress over the past months. He is several times his birth weight. He is no longer mostly horizontal, dependent on being carried or propped up. He is now awake for the majority of the day. He is smiling and laughing, able to recognize members of his family, and babbling confidently. The development both for the baby and for the parents has been so rapid that it is easy to feel that the subsequent years pale relatively into insignificance. The excitement of the first year is over. Now you simply settle down to being a family together, with future development stretching away on a steady continuum. Just as you read the pregnancy books, you have read about the first year. But as for the rest, the progress tends to be thought of as gradual, certainly less visible, and perhaps less exciting.

In fact, although less visibly dramatic than the developments of the first year, enormously important changes continue to take place, particularly in the toddler years. As a result, just as they are beginning to think they are able to settle down to a predictable pattern, parents find themselves having to make adjustments, sometimes as dramatic as those in the first year. For many parents this will come as a surprise. For some it will be met with delight, for others it will be more difficult. This book aims to help parents understand some of this uncharted territory with their toddler.

As in all development, the physical characteristics—that is, the innate bodily givens, the emotional characteristics, and the environment of the child—interweave, determining through their different strands his own particular pattern of progress. For the 1-year-old, the single most important and obvious physical development is the emerging capacity to walk. It is not for nothing that toddlerhood is so called. Toddlerhood is dominated by toddling—the wobbling, unsteady, but upright gait that precedes the acquisition of a fully stable base. Alongside this is the achievement of greater motor control, of both small and large objects, in the environment. From these physical developments stem the major emotional struggles of the second and third years of life: the conflicts with parents over control, the conflicts over separation from the parents, and the conflict between the wish for instant gratification and the demands of reality in the social environment. Of course, such conflicts continue throughout life to a greater or lesser degree, but they reach a particular intensity in the second and third years because the child experiences for the first time his physical capacity to remove himself from his parents. He is no longer utterly dependent on them for movement or feeding. And that is frightening and exciting both for the child and for his parents.

Closely linked to the greater physical potential for separation is the development of language. With better communication the child is also more able to act independently of his parents. Physical closeness is not so critical when language can bridge the gap between the child and his parents. He can also begin to articulate his own wishes and so be more in control of his own environment. At the same time, his better understanding of others' communications means that he is more aware of the restrictions others place on his wishes. But language can help to give him some control over his fierce emotions: he is helped through verbal communication to know that his feelings can be understood and even shared, and he begins to learn to express them.

As the child moves away from his parents more towards the rest of the world, his relationship with himself changes. He starts his second year as king of his environment, the absolute centre of the entire universe, the sun, with his parents as major planets, and family and friends as minor ones, revolving around him. The narcissistic glee with which he greets and entrances others reaches its peak towards the third quarter of the first year. By the end of the second year, through his developing recognition that others have minds and emotions not always unlike his own, he has come to realize that there is competition in his kingdom, that others also have a stake in it. And that some of those others may be bigger and more powerful than he.

Running in parallel with these changes is his growing capacity to play imaginatively and to symbolize the increasingly complex scenarios that he now finds himself part of. From being a 1-year-old playing with and exploring the physical properties of what he can see as well as enjoying peek-a-boo and teasing games, he becomes a 3-year-old who can represent stories both of his own internal experiences and of ones that he has never experienced but can imagine.

For a parent, it can be very confusing time. One minute your child can seem extraordinarily grown up, racing ahead with showing off exciting new physical capacities, running, jumping, climbing with great bravado and pride, and the next minute he is clinging like a terrified limpet unable to move from your side. It is a time when parents often feel trapped and controlled by their children, but also inordinately proud and excited by them. It is a stage that often evokes conflicts of feeling in the parents. How can you both be terrified for the safety of your child as he displays an alarming capacity to run off beyond your reach and your ability to protect him and, simultaneously, feel imprisoned and burdened by the determined tug of the arm as he yet again demands to be lifted up for a carry and a cuddle? As will be seen in chapter 5, battles of will over ownership of his body tend to emerge, especially over feeding, potty training, and getting dressed. One minute he wants you to do it all for him, the next minute he wants to do it completely on his own.

As their child's personality begins to emerge, parents also have to begin to negotiate their own parallel change of role and loss of omnipotence. For some, this will be experienced with sadness as the feelings of warmth generated by the tiny, help-less, dependent baby are replaced by a little more reality as they watch their child growing. Such parents will have to cope with no longer being needed in quite the same way. For others who have been more daunted by their baby's helplessness and vulnerability, their toddler's development will be a relief. His new steps towards the outside world may feel like a reassuring lessening of a burden. These parents may be delighted by the gradual progress towards independence and easier communi-cation. But for most, the new phase will be met with mixed feelings. Sometimes their toddler will delight them. Sometimes he will embarrass them. Sometimes he will disappoint. It is a period that parents often feel turns into a battle of wills as their children try to assert control and independence. Many parents are surprised how they find themselves so easily arguing with their toddlers, almost as if the feelings evoked by their own children turn them (the parents) into toddlers battling for their right to have a say.

Developmental milestones in this period are more public than in the first year. You and your child are probably out and about more than before. It can be a time when parents are watching over their shoulders, looking at the achievements of their children's peers. Often worries that were absent in the first year begin to emerge. You can see and hear what your child is achieving relative to others, and this may throw up anxieties.

This book tells the story of your child's development from being a babe more or less in arms to being a pre-school child, sturdily strong in his own body, ready to turn from parents and the immediate family to embrace the world outside the home. It also tells the story of your own related developments. In telling it, I have avoided using chronological age as much as I can. Children take different steps at different times. For example, some are constitutionally more physical than others at an early age, while others can be more verbal. There is a risk that parents will feel that their child's progress, suddenly so visible and easy to compare, is being set in stone. If he cannot jump by the time he is 2 years old, does this mean he will be hopeless at sport for the rest of his life? If he cannot share, will he always be an aggressive hoarder? If he clings shyly to you, will he never leave home?

The truth is, of course, much more complex. As in infancy, the child's own inborn characteristics interweave with his immediate environment, and with the overall developmental trajectory common to us all, to create the personality. Research shows that the distinction between nature and nurture is not clear-cut: a child's earliest relationships and experiences affect the hard-wiring of his brain very directly, and those changes and developments in his constitution will in their turn, as he grows, influence future interactions with the environment. And such interactions are infinitely varied and subtle.

These variations take place, though, in the context of a body and mind that are, on the whole, programmed to progress along certain developmental lines in the same order, albeit at varied rates. A toddler will not jump before he walks, he will not talk in sentences until after he names objects; learning to share the naming of objects is a precursor to learning to share experiences; alternating tantrums and clinginess precedes more stable independence. There will be variations in the intensity and the ways in which different children negotiate these phases, and children may well meet the challenges in different spheres at different times. But the order in which they move along the trajectories—whether in the realm of their bodies, in their awareness of their and others' minds, in their language, or in their capacity to play—is predictable.

So you will find that although I have avoided chronological age, I follow a pattern of progression over time. And the reassuring fact is that most children, on average, with good-enough help from their parents and the immediate environment, make it through the different stages of these patterns of development to become happily functioning adults. There is not enough room in the world for all the budding stars that parents hope their toddlers will be, but the toddler who did not jump may well enjoy trampolining as a teenager even if he does not enter the Olympics, and the clingy child may soon be playing with peers at school.

Of course, though, you will have an influence over these developments, and this book aims to help you understand your child as you exert that influence. But it is not a counsel of perfection. Indeed, it is particularly important not to be "perfect" for your child as he moves through toddlerhood. A very important part of your role at this stage is to help the toddler adjust to reality, to help him learn to give up his wishes for immediate gratification in favour of behaviour that is more socially acceptable and also safer for his own protection. Inevitably parents find themselves saying "No" a lot at this stage, and it can be a struggle to have to fail him in his expectations of you as you help him adjust to the restrictions of the outside world. But, of course, the main motivator for the child in learning how to be in this wider environment is his love for you. It will be much harder for him to make the necessary adjustments if he is not concerned about the possibility that he may lose your love and approval. The stronger a secure loving and involved base in your relationship built up from the earliest days of his life, the more easily you and he will be able to weather the frustrations and privations, as well as the pleasures, of his move from the cradle through the toddler years. He will monitor your responses to him and change his behaviour accordingly.

But, you may ask, is not this not-too-perfect but "good-enough" parenting, on top of a secure and loving base, a counsel of perfection in itself? I believe not. Rather, it is a counsel of acceptance that there will be times when you get it right and times when you get it wrong; acceptance that, as part of the human race, you will be caught up in conflicts of your own that will affect the way you are with your child, not always in his best interests. We are all victims of our own unconscious internal thought processes and motivations over which we have little control and of which we are unaware. Such influences are unavoidable. They contribute to the diversity of experience in those around us. And, indeed, often it is these same influences that motivate us to have a child in the first place—we may want to be like our parents, or do better than our parents, or compete with our peers—as well as determine the way we behave towards our children once they are with us.

It is important to accept our own ways of relating rather than to feel guilty about them. Guilt can have a corrosive effect, especially during the toddler years, when it is important to remain strong and consistent in the face of provocation and testing of the limits. Much more valuable is understanding, which, in contrast to guilt, can oil the cogs of your relationship. Communication and understanding between people is not straightforward at the best of times, but when one side can articulate only a couple of words and is powered by fundamental instincts, it is perhaps not surprising that it breaks down frequently.

The book aims to increase your understanding. It charts the journey you and your toddler make through different but overlapping realms: the body, the mind, language, symbolization, and play. Of course these arenas overlap with each other extensively, and themes will emerge in common with them all.

Issues of autonomy, separation, and union will criss-cross the chapters. The first and last chapters look at the transitions into and out of toddlerhood, and the chapters in between cover the major themes and issues from the intervening period.

The vignettes are loosely based on the experiences of children and their parents at the Anna Freud Centre toddler groups over many years. Details of identity have been changed. I would like to thank all the toddlers and their parents from whom I have learned so much. They have been my inspiration, and without them this book would not have existed.

on the threshold:
from your arms to their feet

Curiosity and experimentation

Sammy (1 year 1 month)

A smiling exuberant presence, as if in love with what he was now physically capable of achieving, Sammy threw himself into exploring all the toys in the toddler hut, dropping many of them on the floor with delight. Although he hid shyly behind his mother on arrival, he ignored her most of the time. He smiled at any of our contacts with him, as if inviting us to join in his pleasure at what he was doing. Constantly on the go, he moved between the room inside and the garden. He enjoyed pulling the velcroed plastic fruit apart, and the "pizza" pieces, which he then dropped on the floor. Sometimes he played with the wooden spring pop-up figures, putting them in and out of their holes or throwing them, too, on the floor. At other times he wandered around carrying the whole toy, with it dangling from his hand. He took a little aeroplane from another child for a few seconds and then jettisoned it, returning to the pop-up men.

His mother hovered a few inches behind him, anxiously picking up all the toys that had been discarded on the floor. She did not interfere, letting him do what he wanted, laughingly indulging him. She wondered aloud about his disruptive behaviour, though, and was clearly a little embarrassed by the debris that he left in his trail.

Katy (1 year 3 months)
Katy was very busy during the group. She repeatedly climbed onto different little chairs and rather laboriously swivelled herself round to a sitting position, with her feet not quite touching the floor. She looked very precarious as she did this, as if either she or the chairs would overbalance, but she was also very determined and resisted any attempts at helping her. No sooner would she manage to sit down and smile briefly, but with much satisfaction, at her audience than she would slide off and go in search of another chair. Later she became utterly engaged in a determined effort to lift a little shopping trolley up the two steps from the garden into the hut. Again she did this with a driven determination. It was so difficult that she had to sit on the steps to give herself enough leverage to get it through the door. Once she had succeeded, she reversed the process and repeated it several times.

Her mother stood close by patiently watching her but allowing her the space to discover what she could do. She commented on how tiring it was to have a child this age.

Sammy and Katy are typical of toddlers who have just learnt to walk steadily, and their mothers' responses are also characteristic of parents of young toddlers. Such children, so recently upright and so much more in control of their bodies now than a few weeks before, have been described as being in love with the world. Suddenly, from being helpless babies reliant on their carers to mediate between them and their environments, their upright stance allows them the capacity to control their surroundings much better and to manipulate the objects around them They can see the world from all sorts of different angles now: from above and below, upside down and inside out. They appear to spend their lives in continual experimentation. There is a whole new world before them, as they see it with the extra dimensions added. It becomes their oyster. They embrace it with frenetic activity. Much of it resembles scientific experimentation as they concentrate on the impact of their actions and as they explore. Objects are examined for their physical properties—as if the questions the toddler is exploring are: What does this thing do? What shape is it? How does it do it? Does it have an inside and outside? Is it like something I have seen before? What happens when I drop it? The world around them is full of such exciting new objects that they can still get as much pleasure out of the paper that a toy for their first birthday was wrapped in as they do from the toy itself.

At the same time, the toddlers are exploring their own bodies and what their bodies can do. We can see Katy repeatedly and with pride learning to sit on chairs as she has seen others do—she is mimicking those around her, identifying with the bigger people on whom she has been so utterly dependent for the first year of her life. Similarly she is using all her new-found strength and stability to manoeuvre the shopping trolley through the doorway. We can see Sammy's pleasure in controlling the little pop-up men—putting them in and out of the holes, carrying the toy around with him—and in manipulating the velcro fruit.

They are utterly driven by curiosity. It has more intensity than an infant's searching. It is sourced by the newly acquired motor skills and by a fundamental quest we all share to know about our origins and about our place in the world: where do I come from, where do others come from, where and how do I fit in the context I find myself in?

Omnipotence:
the master of the universe

In their exploration of the world around them, Sammy and Katy show considerable disregard for any possible constraints or, indeed, for other people, including, much of the time, their mothers, whom they treat as compliant servants. And indeed, their mothers seem to collude in this disregard, indulging them and supporting them in their quest. Here we are witnessing the intense narcissism of the child in transition from infancy to toddlerhood. Where does this imperious single-mindedness originate?

As babies, our toddlers experienced wishes mostly for food, comfort, or relief from physical discomfort to which, from their point of view, their parents have responded almost magically. Their cries of distress have produced, within a short period of time, some satisfaction of their need. They were hungry, and their feed appeared.

It is not surprising perhaps, then, that the newborn begins to feel that his surrounding environment, particularly in the form of his main caregivers, is there to answer his beck and call. His earliest experiences have taught him that his parents exist for him and for him alone and that he has utter control over them. He learns that there are predictable patterns of response to his actions: he learns over weeks of interactions with his mother that one action on his part will produce another in her, and this gives him a great sense of power over his world. Such self-centred optimism lasts beyond the first birthday. Fortunately it is very seductive. It is hard to resist a 1-year-old's beaming expectation that you will admire his first steps or be delighted to receive from him a chewed and mangled toy when he passes it to you. We encourage his delighted interactions with us, delighting in them as well, and reinforcing his pleasure. His exuberance about what he can do is infectious. He radiates a sense of elation and pride. And, indeed, that elation is almost as rewarding as the knowledge of the first steps themselves. As with so much parenting, it is the shared emotional experience that is as important as the event itself.

Research confirms that this is a period when parent–child interactions are indeed very positive. Scientists have identified the period around the time of learning to walk as being a time of high excitement and exuberance, with generally very positive interactions between parents and their children (only 5%

prohibitory). They have also confirmed it as a period marked by the onset of exploratory behaviour in toddlers. It is thought that the intensity of this exploratory pattern of the early toddler's play, with its accompanying excitement, gives the toddler an enriched experience that in itself contributes further to his development. Interestingly, it seems that children who walk earlier, and are physically more mobile from a younger age, experience greater levels of excitement at this stage than children who walk later. Here we can see how the influence of the physical constitution intertwines with and reinforces emotional experiences in complex ways that in turn influence subsequent development. What happens when, to what, and in which context mingle together to produce the complicated little person growing up so fast in front of your eyes.

Your young toddler's mind

Although Sammy's and Katy's mothers stand back in these observations and let their children get on with their fun in their exploration on their own, both children are aware of their audience. Sammy comes into the room beaming, clearly anticipating our pleasure at seeing him, and Katy looks for her audience and smiles proudly when she sits on the chair. These toddlers know that we can share their pleasure in their experience. Usually some time before their first birthday and well before they start speaking, young children start pointing at objects and then looking at their mothers to see if they are looking too.

Johnny (age 11 months) was being pushed by his mother in the swing. An aeroplane flew overhead. Johnny kicked his feet excitedly and stretched his arm up, pointing up to the sky, and then looked at his mother. She looked up. "Yes. It's an aeroplane", she said, smiling. Johnny continued to look from his mother to the plane and back again, laughing as he did so.

This "joint-attention-seeking" behaviour happens as children begin to understand that their parents can have an interest in something they are interested in, that this interest, as well as the pleasure derived from it, can be shared, and that this sharing of pleasure in itself generates pleasure. It also shows the infant that his mother or father can recognize and respond to his wish for him or her to participate in the experience. In this way, the infant begins to learn about, interpret, and predict the behaviour of others. He is at the very beginning of the long and important process of learning about other people's minds as well as his own. With only a few, if any, words at his disposal at this stage, he is nevertheless beginning to learn about communication through language as well. He very quickly learns that if he points at an object, his mother will look at it too and share his interest and pleasure and that she may even make a predictable sound to go with it. He also soon learns that if he offers her something she will take it, and she may even offer it back to him in return. In this way, social games develop in which the young child is very much in control. In these repeated experiences he is building his own sense of agency— that is, the sense of his own capacity to make things happen, as well as a sense of the "otherness" of the others around him. We look further at these developments in chapters 3 and 4.

Despite the development of these skills in the early stages of learning about his parent's minds, it is important to realize that his understanding of others remains at a basic level. He confidently expects others to cooperate with his wishes as his experience has taught him so far. He does not anticipate any obstacles in the way of getting what he wants. In his interactions with other children, he will take, grab, walk over, and push without any concern for the consequences. In fact, it almost seems as if he treats others as mere objects to be used in whatever way he likes. If he sees a young baby, he will approach it like most other things—as an object to explore.

Johnny (11 months) was sitting in the middle of the laid-out wooden train set that his older brother was playing with. Suddenly Johnny's attention was caught by the noise of another child playing with a tambourine. He crawled towards the musical instruments, oblivious of the train set, knocking it apart as he moved and pushing his brother over in the process, and he laboriously and unsteadily stood up and took the tambourine from the child's hand. Both his brother and the other child looked stunned by Johnny's actions. His brother then broke into a fury, while the child who had been holding the tambourine turned to another toy. Shortly afterwards, Johnny dropped the tambourine and moved away, utterly oblivious to the distress his actions had caused.

It is easy to see that Johnny has yet to think of these other children in these circumstances as anything other than objects that are in the way of what has caught his attention. Unlike older children, he has yet to understand the others as thinking, feeling creatures with desires and wishes of their own. Because they are not able to anticipate that someone else might also want what they have, these young toddlers are not able to understand what sharing means—instead, they just grab what catches their fancy and often immediately discard it. They can be easily distracted by something offering an even more novel and vivid opportunity to explore. Children just a little bit older than them with a more developed sense of others' thoughts, feelings, and intentions will find this behaviour perplexing and puzzling.

The young toddler's emotions

We have already seen how, for many children, this is a period of great exuberance and appropriate self-centredness. It is also a time when parents are needed. Your toddler, in the second half of his first year, will have shown that he recognizes his parents, and those close to him, as special to him. It is likely that he has identified them as the source of the satisfaction of his wishes for comfort and food. Increasingly, as he moves towards his first birthday, other less familiar faces will be unable to comfort him—indeed, they may frighten him. Anxiety about unfamiliar people tends to peak at this time but continues to be present to a greater or lesser extent in many children during toddlerhood. The exclusive need for the familiar face is a dominant feature of the toddler's emotional development. We return to this need in later chapters, especially chapters 2 and 6.

Sometimes, as in the snapshots of Sammy's and Katy's activities, parents are needed only to be ignored or to be left. At other times, as in the case of Johnny, they are there to reinforce the toddler's growing sense of understanding of others' minds. But the continued centrality of the toddler's attachment to and dependence on his parents and main caregivers is crucial. Their levels of pleasure in his pleasure and exuberance reinforce the experience for him and reinforce his attachment to them. And this will be contained in the numerous and subtle interactions between them. Although Sammy and Katy appear to ignore their mothers for much of the time, the presence of their mothers so close to them, recognizing and indulging their wish to explore, is a critical aspect of the scenario. Part of the experiment is "Can I manage without my mother?", but that experiment will fall apart if mother takes herself away from the child for more than a short time. It is the toddler who has to leave the mother in this experiment, and not the other way around.

Children of this age are only just beginning to learn that if someone disappears, they have not been lost forever. When, for example, his mother disappears for any length of time, the baby or young toddler is not able to hold on to an idea of her presence while she is absent. As a result, when he can no longer see his mother, the young toddler will panic, feeling completely alone and abandoned, and there will be desperation in his need to find her again.

Similarly, when things are going badly between him and his mother, it is hard for him to remember simultaneously the good loving mother he also has. It is as if the two images—one hating and one loving—are completely separate, and the one cannot be held in his mind at the same time as the other. Babies and toddlers can easily be overwhelmed and frightened by the intensity of their own fury or by their parents' anger, anxiety, depression, or distress. They easily lose sight of loving feelings at such times. As we shall see, to counter this impression they need repeated experiences of calm, less overwhelming responses from their environment in order to contain their own and what they imagine to be their parents' anger. If a parent instead is punitive and vengeful in response to his or her child's temper, it can confirm the child's sense of overwhelming panic, making him feel increasingly unacceptable and anxious.

Parents of the young toddler

For most parents, watching their child take his first steps is utterly thrilling. Parents mostly feel intense pride and joy at their child's achievements, particularly as he begins to move himself around so confidently. His explorative forays become theirs. It is almost as if they see the world anew through his eyes, and their view of it can become coloured by his enthusiasm. Such pleasure is infectious, and the child picks up on it and, in turn, revels in their delight. These intense, positively charged interactions are important for both his emotional and cognitive development, as we have seen.

But there is another side to this picture. As we can see from Sammy's and Katy's mothers, it is not human to be able to maintain that level of delight constantly, and toddlers also evoke other feelings in their parents. To be a parent of a toddler at any stage of toddlerhood is always demanding. At this stage, your child's confident expectation that you will be the attentive, admiring audience, servant, available for comfort at times of distress, giver and receiver of objects found in the course of exploration, conversationalist, verbal interpreter of his feelings and wishes, and excited participant in his discoveries about the world, as well as continuing to carry out many of the basic caring functions you have done since infancy, may be the source of delight. But it will undoubtedly at times feel like a heavy burden to bear. Both Sammy's and Katy's mothers stood patiently beside their increasingly active children, but Katy's mother articulated the reality for her and for many other parents of children this age: it *is* tiring.

It is unrealistic to expect parents to shadow their toddlers all the time or to be constantly aware whenever their toddlers wish to share their attention to the latest plane in the sky. Parents and caregivers have many other demands on their time. There will be many times when a parent does not meet his or her young toddler's needs in the way that has been described here—he or she may have to answer the telephone or meet a friend or go to an interview for a job—and there will be many times when, even if they try, they will get it wrong for their toddler. They will not understand what he is pointing to, or they will get exasperated or tired by the mess he creates. He will revert quickly from the delighted, seductive optimist to a tired and grouchy needy baby. He will cause havoc with others and cry when he cannot get his way. Dissatisfaction and disagreement will inevitably arise. In fact, it is important that parents do not feel compelled to oblige their toddler at all times. As we shall see in the next few chapters, much of toddlerhood is about parents helping their children to be more realistic in their expectations about the world around them.

As with infancy, what is thought to be important for toddlers in relation to their carers is that when the positive attunement between them is disrupted, the interruption is followed by an attempt to repair it. If misattunement and disagreement is followed by attempts at understanding and adjustment, then even if it is interrupted periodically the child can begin to understand and appreciate the underlying continuity of their parents' attention.

Also, at this point it is likely that not only your toddler but you, too, are beginning to look more outwards towards the world. Now that your child is no longer dependent on you to move around, you may find yourself anticipating a time when he does not need you so much. The temptation in the face of the recognition that soon he will be moving away from you may be to take yourself off first. You may be the kind of parent who has loved having a dependent tiny baby who has eyes only for you—the adoration of a 6-month-old who saves his most ready smiles for his main caregivers is hard to beat—so to sense the end of this phase as your baby begins to take his first steps may be difficult. Some people experience it as the beginning of the end of a love affair. Even if that is not the case, you may nevertheless find yourself looking forward to a new phase where you can have more time for yourself with friends or where your maternity leave has run out and you are having to think about going back to work. You may be impatient, now that your child is apparently moving away, for that phase to start. Others may respond with a pull to keep their children as babies for as long as possible—for example, by finding difficulty either weaning them or moving them into a separate bed.

Other parents may be much happier with a mobile toddler, having disliked the neediness of their babies and having been overwhelmed by their dependence. They may embrace the beginnings of clearer communication with their toddler as he is able to point with huge enthusiasm at what he wants, and they may be delighted at the prospect of a much more active dialogue with their growing child, both verbally and through play.

Whatever the case, changes are often painful as well as pleasurable, and it is sometimes useful for parents to remember that this is a transitional phase for them as well as for their children. Recognizing that they too are having to change and adapt may help some parents identify the wish in themselves to pull away from their toddler prematurely or suddenly when faced with their toddler's activity spurt. This knowledge may allow them to make the adjustments at a gentler pace, more suited to their child's needs. The insight about their own developmental issues may also help parents—particularly those who, for example, long to carry on babying their toddler—to allow him a little more space from them at this stage.

Many parents will feel a mixture of these emotions at different times, and certainly their child's delight will not always coincide with their own—especially for example, in the middle of the night. It is important to remember that this is normal and that your child needs sufficient good-enough emotional interactions with you. He needs to know that what is ruptured can nevertheless be repaired. Most parents provide such a context for their child instinctively. These things are hard to teach. What can interfere with the provision of this good-enough environment is sometimes, paradoxically, terrible guilt about not doing it properly.

Parents who feel guilty about disappointing their child may respond by struggling to avoid that disappointment at all costs, trying to prevent their child from experiencing the very real constraints of the outside world. Not only does the child not learn about the realities of the world, he does not learn that what is ruptured can be regained. He is also likely to pick up on his parents' guilt and on their anxiety about disappointing him. He may be left with a sense of his power over them, which, in turn, itself can cause him much anxiety.

You will find we return to many of these issues later on in the book, particularly in chapter 6.

But my child is not like this

There is huge variability among children, and many will not fit into the picture painted in this chapter. And some may fit into it at some times and not at others. The descriptions here are of the typical developmental pattern of this stage, but, of course, what is also normal is the tremendous range in development both between children and also in the same child over time. Our children are born with different constitutions, and these will naturally affect the ways in which they develop. One child may be naturally much more energetic than another and will be walking and running even before the other can stand unsupported. This will inevitably affect the way they move into the exploratory phase. The more static child may need his parent to help more actively in his quest to find out about the world— or he may become more watchful and observant, using his eyes and ears rather than his limbs to explore. Other children will, during their first year, have had different environmental experiences that will determine the way they approach the transition to toddlerhood. Perhaps illness or a stay in hospital has had an impact on the way they expect their caregivers to respond to them, and they may not have quite the same happy expectation that the world will give them what they want.

But you—his parents and his family—have also provided the context of his first year, and that will have been different and unique for this child—maybe you will have been a little more preoccupied this time round than you were for your other older children, or maybe you have been overjoyed by the arrival of your first at what seems to have been a glittering moment in your life. On the other hand, you may have been depressed following the birth. Perhaps your child comes into a world mixed with joy and sadness because of the loss of another child through miscarriage or because of the loss of a parent.

These events and the feelings they evoke in you around the time of your child's first year will inevitably have an impact on the way you interact with him as he approaches his first birthday. But also equally important, as mentioned in the introduction, are your own core emotional characteristics. These will have intertwined with the different circumstances of his first year and with his innate constitution to make him the wobbling toddler that he is. It is normal for your own early history to influence the way you behave and feel about your children. For example, if you felt neglected as a child or experienced a loss at an early age, you may have an overwhelming wish to protect your own child from such experiences, and this may make it difficult for you to give your child a little more space in which to investigate the world around him. On the other hand, it might make you feel very jealous of your own child's more fortunate babyhood, and you may feel unable to be present for him when his need for you is less consistent. You may be someone who felt very intruded on by your own mother and, as a result, you may find it hard to allow yourself to get too close to your child, for fear of too much intrusion.

We all have personalities and experiences that affect the way we behave with each other and with our children. Fortunately, in most circumstances we have good-enough ways of relating to our children, much of it instinctive, so that the children— mainly, in one way or another—progress through the phases of development described here.

Any individual child may revert back to earlier ways of being, though, when faced with a stressful situation. If Sammy's or Katy's mothers had disappeared from behind their toddlers for any length of time, the children would soon have become the babies they so recently were, in need of physical comfort, to be lifted up and held, possibly to be fed and rocked and caressed until they were certain they had their mothers back again. Such frequent toing-and-froing between different stages of development in any one child is also very typical of toddlers. It makes it hard to know and predict quite what age child you have with you—are they going to be like 4-year-olds or 6-month-olds today?

Moving on

In this chapter, the scene has been set for the newly mobile toddler emerging from his infancy to embark on the beginnings of the journey of discovery of the world around him. We have seen how he will at times embrace this new phase with excitement and seductive omnipotence as he investigates his own body's potential as well as the characteristics of his immediate surroundings. He will need a parent to be present and available, but he also needs to be able to ignore him or her. His experience of her as a thinking, intentional other is emerging but does not yet extend to other children like himself.

2

conflicting passions

The impossible dilemma: together or apart?

In the last chapter we have seen how the 1-year-old both needs his parents and also needs to be able to leave them. We have seen how important it is that they are there in order to be left. The struggle between autonomy from the parents and dependence on them pervades the toddler years, and this intensifies particularly during the second year. As the toddler becomes more aware of his capacity to leave and of the gap that emerges between him and his mother, paradoxically he becomes more aware of his wishes for her. At some point between roughly the ages of 16 months and 3 years, most toddlers will go through a phase of strong feelings of both love and hatred for their parents as they adjust to the fact that they both want and need and do not want to want and need their parents' presence.

This can make it a very confusing and testing time for parents. Often they are reduced to a position where it seems as if nothing they do is right for their child. This is frequently a correct assessment of the situation. Their child finds himself in an impossible dilemma: to get the level of independence he wants and enjoys, he has to leave the parents and act independently; but if he does that, he fears losing them, which is what he dreads most in the world. So he moves closer to them and then feels he is retreating from the opposing pull for autonomy; so he moves away again. Frequently the result is a tantrum, typical of the phase known as "the terrible twos". At times it feels to parents as if the swings of mood and need will never end. They cannot give the toddler what he wants at times of such intense conflict.

It is not unusual for parents themselves to feel intensely ambivalent towards their toddler at this stage. It is not comfortable to be pushed around like a football at any time in one's life, even when the football is a tiny 2-year-old. At such times, the provocation on the part of the toddler towards his parents can be intense. It requires a great deal of patience not to give up and storm off in the face of his conflicting demands for parents both to be there for him and to absent themselves.

As we have seen in the previous chapter, the evidence of the competing pull between greater independence and the need for the parents emerges gradually in the months around the time of the first birthday:

Mother was helping Johnny (1 year 1 month) go down the little slide by holding onto his hands as he slid down. He then saw his older brother go down quickly all by himself, and mother understood that he wanted to manage on his own like his brother. She held onto his hands less and less as he became more confident, and he eventually managed all by himself. He chuckled with glee each time he whizzed down, clearly very pleased with this achievement, and mother stood by looking at him with pride and pleasure.

His older brother fell over and hurt himself, and mother turned to look after him. Johnny appeared oblivious of this, carrying on with his engrossing activity. Soon after, however, mother disappeared inside with his brother. Johnny noticed she had gone and stopped playing. He found it difficult to concentrate on anything much and moved inside too. He

> went towards where she was changing his brother's nappy, but he was content once he could hear her voice; he then settled once again with the toys, even though he could not see her.

Here we see how, in Johnny, the omnipotence and joy of his newly found physical capacities can be dampened by the awareness of distance and separateness. He cannot maintain a sense of mother's presence in her absence. He has to be close enough to hear her. Even many months later, he needs his mother to be present when he panics in the face of an unfamiliar situation:

> Johnny (2 years) was running round and round the room excitedly, but he suddenly stopped when he came face to face with a man he had not met before. He looked at him and then looked at his mother immediately. His mother detected his discomfort and encouraged him to say hello, but Johnny immediately put his hands over his face and made a loud noise. When the man said hello to him, Johnny shrieked "Mummy, Mummy" in a panic and remained with his hands over his face. Mother picked him up, and he snuggled into her chest, putting his thumb in his mouth.

However, not long after, we begin to notice a shift in his attitude to her. It is as if he is beginning to dislike the humiliation of being treated like a dependent baby:

> Mother arrived with Johnny (2 years 1 month), pushing him in the buggy through the rain. He was smiling, apparently eager to be inside the toddler hut. However, as soon as mother picked him up out of the buggy to carry him in, he started kicking and screaming. He refused to come into the room and, continuing to scream and cry, stormed up and down in the little hall, still furious, for many minutes. Mother, after making sure he could not come to any harm, left him and came in on

her own. She sat down beside Johnny's favourite toy, the garage, and started making the lift go up and down with its bell ringing. As Johnny calmed down slightly on his own in the hall, he could hear the familiar sound of the garage lift. He soon ran into the room and went straight to his mother and the garage.

Here, it seems as if Johnny was eager to come to the toddler group, where he already knew it was safe to play at some distance from his mother. Perhaps he wanted to walk in the rain. It seems as if having mother carry him into the hut was too humiliating for him. It took away the autonomy that he was anticipating enjoying, and he reacted with fury as if his very existence were being challenged. However, then he isolated himself in the hall and he lost his mother. It seems as if mother's patience, her recognition of his need to be alone in a safe place, and her use of the attraction of the toy garage allowed him the route to come into the room without losing face.

As we can see, in just a few weeks an older child is likely to be more determined in his wish to be independent of his mother. He will feel and hope that he does not need her and does not want to be treated like a baby any more. He puts a distance between them but then feels lost, in need of his source of feelings of safety, but then hates his dependence.

Learning about "No"

But these crises over dependence and independence are not the only sources of conflict at this stage. Compounding the struggles for the toddler and his parents are battles between his wishes for the kind of immediate gratification he so recently experienced as a baby and concerns for his safety, now that he is so much more adventurous with his higher levels of activity and, as well, the social constraints beginning to be imposed by the outside world. Parents will find as their toddler moves towards his second birthday that they are increasingly having to say "No". Research has shown that at around 20 months, as much as three-quarters of parental interactions with their children are prohibitions of one kind or another.

The combination of physical activity and bravado frequently puts the toddler of this age in very unsafe situations. He can run now, often quite fast, but, apart from concern about losing you, he has no sense of the dangers that exist in the environment. He has to learn from you about the risks of cars and roads, about the dangers of climbing too high, about not throwing or crashing his toys too forcefully. Not hurting himself or other people is something that he has to learn, and you are the most important teacher that he has. This can be difficult when his pleasure in what he can achieve now is so intense and his response to your prohibitions is so furious. Many parents also worry that they may instil too much fear, turning their children into being overcautious and unwilling to experiment with the full potential of what their bodies can do. Other parents may inadvertently overexcite their child and expose him to greater physical dangers than they need to because they (the parents) get such vicarious pleasure from the child's intense excitement. Finding the right balance can be hard, but at stake is your toddler's capacity to feel safe, confident, and more in control of his body.

But it is not just physical dangers that lead parents to curb their toddler's wishes. Growing up is also about learning to adapt behaviour to levels of social acceptability. It would be impossible to live together in a world where everyone indulged in babyhood wishes for instant results. We have to learn to postpone or forego our infantile wishes. We cannot continue to expect to be fed on demand, to take things just because we want them, to evacuate our bodies whenever the urge takes us. We all have to learn in childhood about sharing, about delaying wishes, about controlling our bodily functions.

This is a hard lesson for a toddler to learn. Why should he, just because his parents say, give up what seemed so recently to be his birthright? Inevitably, our so recently king-of-all-he-surveys will feel humiliated and disappointed. There he was thinking that his wishes were paramount, and now he finds they have to be compromised. It is not surprising that the dethroning is accompanied by a struggle. Tantrums are inevitable:

Johnny (2 years 1 month) was engrossed in playing with water at the sink. His mother told him it was time to stop because it was home time. She emptied the bowl of water, while he shouted "No". He got very angry and refused to cooperate while she tried to change him out of his by now wet clothes. He threw himself on the floor, thrashing and screaming, and seemed not to know any more what he was so upset about. Mother struggled calmly to get enough clothes on him to keep him warm for the journey home, explaining to him that she understood how hard it was to stop when he was having such fun. Eventually, between the wails, he said goodbye.

Even children who have, on the face of it, taken on board the need to comply with their parents' injunctions regress to expressing their fury about the predicament they are being put in:

Jodie (2 years 2 months) was usually extremely quiet and cooperative, learning early to say please and thank you when prompted by mother. However, at one snack time she very clearly expressed her resentment at the constraints her mother and others placed on her. Uncharacteristically she grabbed a breadstick even before it was put on the table, and she refused to say please. She then refused to sit at the table, despite mother's efforts to put her on a chair, and eventually was so angry that she threw herself full length on the floor and would not allow mother to touch her. Mother sat near her while she calmed down and acknowledged that she had probably been wrong to be so insistent at the point where Jodie wanted to assert her independence, remarking that you clearly have to choose your battles and that this was not one that was so important.

In both these situations, the mothers eventually recognized their children's need for independence and for control. They did not let their toddler's fierce opposition to them enrage them, but, instead, reflected on what they (the mothers) had not got quite right for their children. This gave them the space to see things more from the point of view of their child and allowed them calmly to respond to the child as he or she came out of the tantrum.

It is important to recognize that the conflicts between your child's simultaneous wishes for autonomy and distance, between his wish for activity and his need for safety, and between his wishes for instant gratification and the demands of the social world we live in are all part of the normal course of development for him. The anger that accompanies the struggle is an inevitable consequence of the ambivalence towards you that these conflicts engender in him. That love and hatred for the same person can coexist is hard at times for many of us to accept. It is no wonder that it drives our toddlers to such extremes of emotion.

Love and hate

It is not uncommon for toddlers to express their mixed feelings towards you in very direct ways. Biting, for example, may be accompanied both by feelings of wanting to be so close as to want eat you up as well as of wanting to destroy and inflict pain. Hair pulling could be seen in the same vein. In both these examples what starts off as affectionate quickly collapses into being aggressive, and we see the release of the tension of love and hate, the feelings of "I want you/don't want you".

Other toddlers may find it much harder to express their negative feelings. Their ambivalence goes underground as they withdraw into compliance. Their placating behaviour may reflect a feeling that their mother cannot tolerate their aggression and that it must not be shown.

The mother of Peter (2 years 4 months) was very depressed and became upset talking about her difficulties to another mother. Peter observed his mother carefully during the conversation and then went to play with the teddy-bear puzzle, which had faces with different moods on them. He switched them around and changed their moods. He looked sad and solemn. His baby brother started to cry suddenly. His mother suggested Peter give him a kiss. He ran over to him and did so, returning to enjoy his mother's praise.

Here it is possible to speculate that Peter was aware of his mother's vulnerability and precarious state. He had no choice but to obey his mother's wishes—to get angry with his brother would have been too dangerous for his mother to bear.

Sometimes a child who, for whatever reason, thinks it is unacceptable to express negative feelings will dissociate, appearing withdrawn, blank, and unemotional as if he is not allowed to feel anything at all. Other children may respond by expressing their aggression more indirectly—for example, by becoming withholding. This withholding may come in many forms: of their bodies, of their affection, of their appetite, or of their faeces (see chapter 5). Alternatively they may develop other ways to wind their parents up—for example, by playing in ways that are unsafe and becoming accident-prone. The risk is that any of these less direct ways of expressing their ambivalent feelings may harm their progress. To become withdrawn, withholding, over-placatory, or accident-prone, for example, may have a detrimental influence on a child's capacity to engage in subsequent relationships. If he has to disguise his authentic experience because of its impact on his parent(s), then he may feel less confident about his own overall accept-ability. The toddler will be depriving himself of part of a normal experience and, in the process, may be retreating to a position where his overall development suffers.

In struggles such as these, parents often wonder how they will ever manage to influence the will of their imperious little child. It is very easy to lose sight of his difficult dilemmas and to feel instead that the tantrums are a sign that he is being straightforwardly naughty. Sometimes parents feel that their child is deliberately malicious towards them, and they may feel inclined to punish him harshly. What often takes parents by surprise is the strength of their own reaction to the position the toddler puts them in. They find themselves reduced to their own toddler-like feelings of swings between love and hate, one minute wanting to escape from their child and the next minute wanting to kiss and cuddle him. They can find themselves being inconsistent and giving their child confusing mixed messages:

Johnny (1 year 11 months) and his mother were building towers out of the beakers. Johnny managed to build a small one with three beakers, and he looked at his mother proudly. "Well done", she praised him. He then tipped over the top beaker of the tower and looked at her expectantly. She then started laughing and helped him tip the other two beakers onto the table. He laughed excitedly and swept all three beakers with force onto the floor. "No Johnny. It's tidy up time. Don't do that", she said disapprovingly. He looked at her, clearly puzzled.

In this entirely commonplace exchange between Johnny and his mother, it is possible to see how easy it is to muddle one's child. As with all our interactions, it is impossible to get them right all the time. What is important is to keep on trying and to repair and rebuild the communication between you.

Toddlers need your help in regulating their feelings. They need to feel safe enough with their anger that it is not utterly overwhelming. Both mothers of our screaming toddlers helped their child know that they understood their feelings but did not appreciate the way they were expressing them; in verbalizing their feelings for them, they were modelling an alternative way to be. They also knew that their children were safe, but they did not give them any positive reinforcement for their unacceptable behaviour. The children nevertheless knew that their mothers were not vengeful, could indeed admit to their own inadequacies in the situation, and would take them back when they (the toddlers) had calmed down and were ready. The mothers conveyed a sense to their toddlers that their (the toddlers') interactions could be different and a confidence that their children would come out of their tempers.

The capacity of the toddler to better regulate his emotions as he moves towards his third birthday is explored further in our final chapter. In the next chapter we look in more detail at the changes in the toddler's awareness of other people and of others' minds and emotions and at how that affects his own feelings towards and about them.

3

learning about
their mind and yours

Trying to understand each other:
thoughts and feelings

Being able to monitor our own and other people's feelings about us is an essential part of our everyday lives. Without this capacity it would be very hard to function in a social world. Your feelings about other people and also your feelings about their feelings about you are essential ingredients in all communication. They are reflected in our body movements as well as in the ways we talk to and about each other. They influence the way we learn, what motivates us, our work, our play, and our friendships. We interact with each other all the time on the basis that we can assume what is going on in another's mind. We do not always get it right, of course, and that can lead to misunderstandings, but it does not stop us from functioning on the basis that, on the whole, we do have some sense of what others are thinking or feeling. And we acquire that sense from our previous experiences.

Throughout childhood we gradually learn about the important realm of interpreting other people's thinking and feeling minds and of distinguishing them from their actions and behaviour. In order to do this we have to learn about our own minds too. Such learning is not factual. It is experiential. It takes place in an emotional, feeling context, and it takes place unconsciously. We are not aware that we are doing it. No one can consciously learn these things. They are embedded in our implicit memories, giving us a sense of just being part of what we are.

Children acquire the capacity to recognize their own—and others'—imagining and feeling minds through the experience of repeated minute and subtle interactions with those close to them, primarily their parents or their main caregivers. There will be many mistakes and frequent misunderstandings in these repeated interactions, but the important ingredient is the continued search for mutual understanding. It is known that children with parents who, rather than only considering what their child is doing, consider what he is thinking, feeling, and wishing do much better themselves in later life at understanding what lies behind the behaviour of others. Much of this learning happens during the toddler years. Your toddler will go through a huge shift in the way he understands his own and other people's thoughts feelings and behaviours by the time he is 3 years old.

Here is Julia, aged 2 years 10 months:

Christopher was crying loudly and continuously. Julia stopped playing with the doll's house and stared at him, looking worried. She asked her mother if he had hurt himself. Later, at tidy up time, Mary was crying. Julia told us, "She does not want to go home".

For Julia to be able to articulate feelings on behalf of another child, she must have an awareness of herself as someone who has feelings that are reflected in her actions, and she must also be aware of other children as having thinking, feeling minds like her. She knows what it is like to be unhappy if you have hurt yourself or are sad when it is time to go home, and she assumes that the other children are feeling the same as she would in those circumstances. This is a huge achievement and is in very marked contrast to our 1-year-old Johnny (chapter 1) who, you may remember, treats other children as if they are almost part of the furniture, as inanimate objects, to be pushed, pulled, and grabbed, without a thought for their emotional responses.

Learning from you

At around their first birthday, children are often fascinated by the inside and outsides of objects. They will play with containers for hours—looking inside and outside beakers and bottles, exploring inside and outside their and other people's mouths, noses, ears, handbags, boxes, briefcases. As they become more mobile, they can see the world from different angles. Once you can crawl under a table or around a chair, it looks very different from the way it looked when you were only able to see it from a fixed, lying-down or sitting-up position. In their newly acquired mobile exploration, young toddlers are learning that the same object can look different from different angles—that even though the table is quite different looking from below, it is still the same table. That a beaker is the same object inside and out. And that people have insides as well as outsides. They are learning that all objects have different dimensions. That what you see is not the totality of what you get. That there is more to the world than meets the eye. And in a sense, this is what they are learning about in themselves and in those close to them—that they have internal worlds and that those close to them do too.

This process starts from the first days of your baby's life. From the very earliest "conversations" you have had with him, long before he can talk, you will have been attributing thoughts and feelings to him that explain his behaviour to you. You will have told him he was crying because he was hungry or had a tummy ache, you may have said he was cross because you were too busy to feed him at that moment, or you may have said he was happy to see the mobile hanging from the ceiling. In this way he learns from your treatment of him as a thinking, emotional being whose actions reflect an inner state of mind. He learns about his own mind from how you relate to it. He learns about himself and his wishes from the meanings attributed to his behaviour by you. This process then becomes reciprocal as he, in turn, learns about your wishes and motivations underlying your behaviour. Later, in more verbal play, as your baby begins to babble, smile, and laugh during the course of his first year, he will experience you as someone with whom it is possible to have shared experiences of pleasure. In your responsiveness and involvement and admiration, he learns that you have a feeling mind. He will also start referring to you in situations that are strange to see how you are reacting, as if trying to work out from your response whether it is a situation you are happy or unhappy in and, from that, will learn about it. A positive response from you will allow him to explore further, while a negative response will make him much more inhibited. When a toddler does this "social referencing", he is acknowledging, at some level, that you his parents have information that is different from his and that will help to guide him in his responses.

Building a sense of otherness

We have seen how the toddler advances over the threshold from infancy with primarily self-centred views. King of all he surveys, the world revolves entirely around him. Other people and animals may be objects of curiosity to be explored, and they may seem different because they move, but there is no consciousness of them as experiencing beings. Only his parents and other close familiar faces are acknowledged as individuals who might have different intentions from him, but even then his experience and expectation is that he can quickly draw their attention back to him.

Gradually, though, he has been building a sense of the otherness of those close to him. As we have seen, although still very self-centred, he has become aware that his mother is not entirely an extension of his own wishes. Slowly he has become aware of his own and his mother's separate senses of agency. He learns that he can point and that subsequently others will look, and may point too, and that in doing that he can effect change in other people's actions. He has agency. They have agency. And he and they can influence each other.

At the start of his second year, the toddler's developing capacities include beginning to be able to understand that his closest carers have feelings that are distinct from his own and the knowledge that he and they can influence each other's behaviour through shared communication. As the year progresses, these capacities extend to recognition both that others can have thoughts and desires that are different from his own and that these characteristics are true of the wider world, not just of his parents and close carers. During this year, as the toddler begins to be aware that, as well as him leaving mother, she can become lost, he is also starting to respond to others and not just his main caregivers in ways that suggest he can attribute desires and wishes to them.

Increasingly aware by now that he cannot omnipotently control his parents, that he is not king of all he surveys, he simultaneously has to confront the knowledge that the world, formerly his oyster, is peopled by others with desires and wishes similar to his own. At this stage, the toddler's disillusion can be intense.

Here is Mary at 17 months, on the cusp of having to acknowledge others' desires:

> Mary came to the group with her father after a break of a few weeks. As usual, she made straight for what had always been her little empire, the dolls and the dolls' bed and buggies, and busied herself and father with them. One of the new children

came over and took one of the dolls and a buggy from her and walked away with them. Mary did not protest but stared after the child for a long time, looking dazed and puzzled. After a while she returned to playing with the dolls, instructing her father to dress them. Later, at snack time, for the first time Mary refused to join the other children at the table, crying vehemently in protest when father tried to pick her up to take her there. Eventually, when all the children except one had left the table, she could not resist the banana and sat down, indicating the seat beside her for her father. She spent the whole session looking very wide-eyed, solemn, and vigilant, in strong contrast to the weeks before the break, when she had invariably been utterly engrossed in her play and oblivious of much apart from the dolls and her mother.

In this snapshot, it is possible to speculate that not only has Mary to come to terms that day with her mother not being available for her beck and call, even though father is, but also that she has to accept that other children may have wishes that do not coincide with hers—wishes that, indeed, may be in direct conflict with hers. A few months later:

Mary was on her own playing in the "kitchen" with the "pizza", trying to cut it up with a "knife". John approached the table and made as if to take the knife from Mary. She grabbed hold of it even more firmly, stopping what she was doing and staring hard at him defiantly. Mary's mother told her she had to share it with John. Fortunately there was another "knife" nearby, and John quite happily took that. Mary resumed her cutting briefly and then moved away.

Here we can see that Mary has learnt to anticipate John's wishes. She is prepared through previous experiences of his snatching of what she has, and she grabs on to it even before he tries to take it. It seems as if Mary already has some awareness of her own possessive wishes and is beginning to be aware of the possibility of possessive wishes in others. It is at this stage that parents begin to worry about their child's ability to share—they are suddenly exposed to their toddler's possessiveness and their toddler's awareness of that in other children's minds. It is important to remember that this is a significant part of their development, and their possessive reaction is in many ways understandable. The ability to share is not an innate behaviour but something that has to be learned in the face of a developing awareness of others' wishes and desires.

By the time she is 3 years old, it is likely that Mary's awareness of others' minds will have extended to the capacity to understand and articulate other children's emotional responses, as Julia did, in terms of their wishes and desires: "She is crying because she does not want to go home."

Misunderstandings

At the root of this developing capability in toddlers is the nature of their emotional relationships with those close to them. Beliefs about others and about what they feel and believe are dependent on the toddlers' experiences of their relationships with those closest to them. Parents who are less able to reflect and feed back to their child the nature of their own thoughts and feelings as well as their thoughts about their child's thoughts and feelings will make it harder for their child to be reflective about others. Sometimes, for example, parents find it difficult to allow their child a sense of his own agency, instead being tempted to take over his activities, imposing their own meaning on his actions rather than struggling to find the meaning to him.

Joe (1 year 2 months) crawled back towards mother, who had been frantically trying to distract him from going outside. She tried to get him interested in a hat, saying, "This is a hat, and it is spelled "h-a-t". He soon crawled away to the ball toy. He copied the toddler leader, who showed him how it worked. Mother compared the colours of the balls, demonstrating the green one which was like a green brush nearby. He crawled towards the truck, but mother persisted with the colours.

Here we can see a mother who, in her enthusiasm to teach her son, does not understand the importance to him of trying to understand the meaning and the feelings expressed behind his actions: perhaps, for example, that he wants to explore, that he does not want to be inside, that he likes toys that move. She and he are missing out on the opportunity to learn that behaviour has underlying meaning that can be interpreted, articulated, and understood.

In this vignette, the very common concern on the mother's part to educate has interfered with the much more important and age-appropriate need for reflective understanding of the toddler's internal world. Other parents may be too ill, preoccupied, absent, or depressed to be able to focus much on understanding the meaning of their child's behaviour, and inevitably this will have an effect on their child's capacity then to understand others.

A toddler who has had an experience of a parent who is severely mentally ill, violent, or abusive may find the experience of knowing about another's thoughts or wishes too frightening or dangerous. In this way, the toddler will develop only a minimal capacity to attribute thoughts to others, and the wish to understand others' minds may be seriously impaired. This will have a profound effect on the toddler's subsequent capacity to relate to others.

Of course, our ability to be completely attuned all the time to our toddler's behaviour is never perfect, and nor should it be. Inevitably, we are all preoccupied part of the time and will not be available. Also, everyone's capacity to understand the meaning of their toddler's actions will, in turn, be affected by their own experiences of close relationships in their childhood. The thoughts and feelings we attribute to our children will inevitably be influenced by our own thoughts and feelings. Misunderstandings and mistakes will occur, but what is important is that a channel of communication remains open. Then the mistakes and misunderstandings, and the responses to those mistakes and misunderstandings, can be understood together.

play and language

Your child's toddler years are characterized by a flowering of his capacity to play and to begin to use language. Playing and language provide a link between you. Both of them are ways for the child to bridge the emerging gap as he acquires the physical capacity to move away from you. But that sense of coming together in mutual understanding through play or language also acts, for the child, as a catalyst for further separation—they are a route for communication and interaction with the outside world.

Early images and games: coping with what's missing

A child's ability to play and to talk stems from his being able to symbolize, to make one thing stand for another: a doll represents a baby, a stethoscope a doctor, the word "table" stands for the object table. We can speculate that from his earliest days a baby has been able to conjure up images of things in their absence. When he cried for his mother to feed or comfort him, it is likely that after repeated experiences of relief from the bodily discomfort he began to be able to hold an image of an anticipated response to his cries that is missing until it appears. Babies of quite a young age will often stop crying when they hear the sounds of their feed being prepared or the sound of their mother's voice. In a sense, these images of what is missing can be thought of as early forms of symbolization, and as time goes on and parents become slightly less adaptive to their baby's needs, the baby will begin to rely on these images as sources of comfort to fill the gap between his wishes and the satisfaction of those wishes. In some cases he may even create his own physical "symbols" of the experience of his mother's comfort in her absence by thumb-sucking or finding a piece of soft material to soothe himself. When he plays peek-a-boo, the baby's pleasure stems from the reappearance of a familiar face that, for that brief moment of absence, he has been able to hold as an image in his mind. What is more, even at this very early age the baby's delight in this game of predictable, controllable appearance and disappearance would seem to indicate that he at some level "knows" that the repeated disappearances are not for real. If they were, then he would become distressed.

As we have seen in the previous chapter, as he approaches his first birthday the baby begins to become aware that his parent and he can have independent relationships to a third object. He begins to learn that there is a perspective on the world that is different from his own. At this stage not only will babies start to look to their parents for guidance about how to feel about an outside situation or person, and start to draw their parent's attention to outside objects and witness their responses to them, they will also begin to initiate games of giving and receiving other objects. It is as if in these teasing games of mutual exchange the baby is symbolizing his own experience of having wishes frustrated and unfulfilled and then having them fulfilled, and as if in some way he is watching the other's experience of such transactions.

Exploratory play

These early games, where we can see the emergence of a capacity for imagination and symbolization in the growing, more mobile pre-toddler, are mostly centred around familiar caring relationships. But, as we saw in chapter 2, much of the activity of the toddler on the threshold of walking will be exploratory play where symbolization is less evident. Instead, the toddler is busy satisfying the tremendous curiosity, which pervades this stage, about the properties of his environment and of his and others' bodies.

In the following snapshots of Katy's play, only a few weeks apart, it is possible to see her progression from being the little scientist with her toys to being able to use the same toys as symbols for the real thing in what is becoming pretend play.

Katy (1 year 2 months) stood at the little table pulling apart the plastic fruit in a mechanical way and allowing the pieces to fall on the floor. Although the toddler assistant named the fruit, Katy seemed interested only in the noise the Velcro made as it tore apart and in the process of dividing it. Her mother asked the staff if they thought she knew it was pretend fruit. A slightly older child came in and started "cooking" with the fruit. Katy watched her for a few seconds and then, apparently uninterested, turned away.

A few weeks later:

She was standing at the little table picking up the Velcroed plastic fruit. She pulled it apart and then looked across at her mother. She put the "apple" to her mouth and said "nyum, nyum, nyum", making smacking noises with her lips. Her mother asked if it was an apple.

Accepting your toddler's play

In these examples it is also possible to see the role that the adults around Katy assume when interacting with her: they accept her play and, at the same time, extend it just a little bit further. In the first example, even though Katy appears uninterested, the assistant tells her the names of the fruit; in the second one, mother asks if it is an apple. This pattern of mother meeting child, being attuned to the child in their activities, and then extending the activity a little further (some have called it inexact mirroring) exists typically in interactions between parent and child from birth onwards. We see it in "baby talk", in social referencing, in joint attention-seeking, in early conversations, and in pre-school elaborate pretend play. Mothers or other significant adults will listen to the messages from the child, whether verbal or gestural, let the child know they are being understood and heard, and then try to take that understanding a little further in the child. For example, when Johnny, in chapter 1, pointed at the aeroplane, his mother said "Yes it's an aeroplane", even though he did not have any words at that stage. It is as if parents assume and attribute understanding to their child's activities well before the child is able to express that understanding.

A very important ingredient in the development of play is our acceptance of our toddlers' games and their pretend world. Just as we know not to challenge their precious piece of comforting blanket, we do not break their illusory world by telling them it is not true. In this way we can help them have an illusion of being linked together with us through the game, and this shared state then allows them to practise being separate.

In the following vignette we can see Lizzie, who was a late walker and has mostly played with dolls very close to her mother, making the most of an opportunity to explore safely a space slightly more distant from her mother than she has been used to:

Lizzie (1 year 6 months), who had only just learnt to walk unaided, was playing in the kitchen with the toddler assistant, who was exaggeratedly drinking from the cups and stirring them as well as pouring from the teapot. The toddler assistant wondered if Mummy, who was sitting on the other side of the room, would like some. Lizzie solemnly and seriously grabbed the teapot and a cup and walked unaided, stretching out her arms to near her mother to give her the pot and cup, to which mother responded gratefully as if she were thirsty; but Lizzie did not get too close to her, and then she walked back to the assistant at the table. She did this a couple of times.

Together and apart

A huge amount of toddlers' play is about separation; about losing and re-finding someone or something. Freud wrote about this in his description of his great-nephew's game of throwing a cotton reel over the side of his cot over and over again, saying "gone" and "back" each time. The little boy's mother had just gone out, and Freud recognized that the toddler was probably protecting himself from her absence by doing to the cotton reel what was done to him: "I do not need you; I am sending you away myself." In this way he gives himself the pleasurable experience of being grown up, of doing what grown ups do, and hands over the disagreeable experience of being a small abandoned child to someone or something else. There are innumerable ways in which children rehearse the experience of things coming and going—their fascination with doors opening and closing, with shapes that disappear as they are posted through holes, with toy tunnels that toy trains disappear into or bigger tunnels that children can disappear into, and then, as they get older, with games of hide-and-seek. Even their pleasure in balls rolling or cars that are pushed between two people can be seen as practising linking and then separating from another person.

An important part of the pleasure in these games is the relief at being reunited following separation. The experience of being apart is mastered. What is done to the toddler in real life is done to the toys or other characters in the pretend experience.

Toddlers can also use their play to help them get over more difficult experiences. For example, a toddler who has seen a car accident might play repeatedly in a push-a-long car, making it stop or "crash". He could be helped, if he does not think of doing it himself, with encouragement to find tools to fix the car. Visits to the doctor or the hospital that frighten your toddler can be helped by games with a "medical kit" that the child can explore and use to treat dolls or other people. Such games can, however, be difficult for parents anxious about a very sick child. It can be tempting in these situations to cope with our own painful adult feelings by assuming that our toddler is better off not being exposed to any knowledge of the forthcoming treatment, even if it is through play. However, the child will benefit from the opportunity to anticipate, familiarize, and master the frightening procedure in hospital just as he does with playing out the car accident he saw.

Expressing feelings through play

Parents sometimes find the content of their children's play rather shockingly direct. They may find it hard when their peaceful son or daughter starts to make the tiger attack all the farm animals or when the cars come crashing down the garage ramp onto the floor. They may not like it when their toddler succeeds in building a tower of bricks very carefully and then suddenly swipes it down. It is important, though, to remember that children often express unacceptable feelings in their play, much to their pleasure, just as we sometimes get pleasure from the expression of unacceptable feelings in our "play"—such as card or board games where it is legitimate to wipe out our opponent, or viewing films or reading books where all sorts of violent activity takes place and we enjoy seeing the "pretend" hero commit all sorts of unacceptably violent and shocking acts. And simultaneously, as with toddlers and their games, we are able to master our anxiety, turning our fear of being a passive victim into an experience of active power and absolute control.

Katy (2 years 10 months), normally a polite and compliant child, was tired from a morning at her new nursery, and she and mother had had an argument about her having to change out of her school clothes. She played with the tiger, among all the farm animals. Mother asked what the tiger eats, and Katy paused for a moment and then said "you". Mother laughed, and Katy said "He hates you". Mother was puzzled and asked "Ate or Hates?" and Katy said "He hates you". Mother asked what she could do to make the tiger like her again, and they resumed talking about and looking at the other farm animals.

Through the tiger's voice, Katy takes control and expresses her resentment of her mother. Her mother in turn accepts her daughter's pretend world and joins in by acknowledging the tiger's angry feelings and trying to help find resolution.

Playing with your child

Your toddler then learns about the world and about others as well as himself and about emotions and relationships between others and himself through play. It is critically important for his development that he acquires the capacity to play. As parents you can do much to encourage it, just as Katy's mother did. This does not mean that you have to actively take over his games—or even to get totally absorbed in his play. It is more important to be available to be used in his games as he likes and to let him know occasionally that you are there and willing to participate. You might want to extend his ideas just a little, but it is very important that he owns the game and that it does not become yours. For many parents this will come naturally, but for some it will be more difficult. It is not always easy for parents to play with their children. Not only are there important practical issues like time availability, but parents' own emotions may also make it hard to join in.

It may be, for example, that you had very little opportunity to play yourself as a child and that you feel ignorant about how to go about playing with your toddler. Sometimes people feel foolish to be seen playing with their child—their toddler's passionate primitive feelings or preoccupations that are revealed in play seem to them to be embarrassing. Instead, they may prefer to educate their child in ways that, in fact, cut across the child's own readiness to explore in playful ways:

Rebecca (1 year 8 months) took a toy cow and tried to put it in a little cot. Her mother said it was far too big, and anyway cows did not sleep in beds.

Sometimes—strange though it may seem, and often people are unaware of it—people can even be envious of their child's freedom and pleasure, and this can interfere in their ability to become involved or even to allow their child to play. Other parents may be sad to lose their dependent, involved baby and are reluctant to allow them the space in which to develop ideas of their own and to experiment in play.

Richard (2 years) was wandering around the room waving a toy broom vaguely in the air. Father told the staff they had had a terrible night with him—he had woken several times— and father said he (father) was exhausted. He looked very tense. He trailed Richard, anxiously hovering over him, saying he was worried he might hit someone. Soon he took the broom away from him.

It is possible to see in this snapshot how, perhaps understandably, one father's exhausted and angry mood made him miss an opportunity to encourage his son to pretend with the broom in a way that might have absorbed the toddler and allowed him to see the potential to use the broom in a way that would not involve hitting someone. Instead, the father sees his son as being as angry as he is and straight away suspects him of aggression. As we have seen, it is all too easy to attribute our own emotions to our children. You would not be human if similar feelings to Richard's father did not sometimes interfere with your relationships with your children, but it is important both to try to remember that they do have a separate independent emotional life from yours and to try to encourage them in their exploratory games. One of the greatest achievements you can help generate in your toddler is the capacity to play creatively and with pleasure.

Language

Your child's first truly intelligible words will probably occur around the time of his first birthday, just as he is beginning to become more aware of his separateness from you. Often the first words coincide with his joint attention-seeking behaviour (chapter 1)—that is, the awareness that he and you can have a relationship with a third object in the world and he can draw your attention to it. To begin with your baby will do this by gesturing, but increasingly he will discover that how he vocalizes can have an effect on your attention. He is learning that the world does not centre entirely round him, but simultaneously he is acquiring the elements of a sense of agency—he can influence others in their actions, and he can do it using the sounds he can make, just as he is influenced by the sounds that others direct towards him. And just as you become more confident with him and slightly less adaptive to his every wish by, for example, encouraging him to wait for his feeds, his greater mobility is allowing him to be physically more distant from you. In these circumstances, the use of voice and sound becomes a good way to cross the increasing physical gap that is emerging between you. Your voice and his voice allow you to maintain contact round corners, in the dark, or with your backs to each other! In the example of Johnny, aged 1 year 1 month, in chapter 2 who had to search for his mother following her sudden disappearance, it is possible to see how just the sound of mother's voice is enough to soothe him so that he can go off and play on his own for a while.

Your young toddler is beginning to learn, too, that in the absence of your close physical presence, his wishes can be expressed by making sounds—he can "speak" and you will respond. This pattern of interaction between you has had its roots in your earlier games when he was quite small and you "talked" to his babble, when you imagined and gave meanings to his incomprehensible, very first sounds. It is through your early conversations with him, through your understanding and vocalizing of what you thought he was telling you, that he comes to understand that you can share experiences and the expression of those experiences with him.

As he begins saying his very first words, you will find that there are many times when you will not always understand what he means. You will often struggle to get it right. Communication with a toddler is not always straightforward, and often there is no apparent correct meaning—there may be many possible meanings to what your toddler is trying to say. But the important thing is to keep trying—your repeated search and expectation that what he has tried to vocalize is meaningful is what is significant to his development.

The more you talk with him and allow him to know that you are treating his attempt at communication as meaningful, the more he will try to communicate using words. Most parents do this instinctively. Research has confirmed that most parents take what their child is saying and just push it a little further by saying a bit more, by adding to what their toddler says. They extend the child's narrative to slightly beyond what the child is expressing. It is as if parents know instinctively that their children can absorb and understand more than they can express. If Johnny (chapter 1), who pointed to the plane, had been a little older and had also said "plane", then mother might well have expanded the experience by trying to develop a shared story about the plane. "Yes. It's flying in the sky. I wonder where it is going. Is it going to see Granny?" In this way she is showing her son that she can share his interest, that they can understand the world together, and that they can share the meanings of words about it.

As your toddler gets older and more confident with language, and as his cognitive capacities develop, he will move from using single words to name objects and people in his immediate environment to stringing a couple of words together. He is then more clearly able to express his wishes— "more juice" or "no bye-bye", for example. And as parents you will find yourselves, as you used to earlier, carrying forward the conversation, repeating it back to him in a slightly different form perhaps, and then encouraging him to add to it—"You don't want to leave now, but it is going home time", to which the child may echo "going home time".

Language and coping

Children of this age are beginning to use language to express internal states of mind. "No bye-bye" expresses a wish not to leave, which the parent rightly interprets, implying shared understanding at the toddler's regret and recognition of his conflict. Even at a very young age, when only on the cusp of playing symbolically with dolls and barely talking, one child momentarily mimics her mother's caring for a baby in need of comfort:

Sandra (1 year 4 months) tried and failed to fit herself into the little doll's buggy. Encouraged by her mother she puts a doll into it instead, and, covering it up, she bends down close to it and says "aah".

Increasingly your toddler will begin to link words with inner experiences and, in the process of doing so, will be better able to handle those experiences.

Simon (2 years 2 months) was playing with the toy cars and planes. He said "helicopter" as he handed the toddler assistant one of the helicopters. Then he handed over a broken helicopter and looked expectantly as if to ask if it could be repaired. When told it couldn't be, he said "broken helicopter" quite peacefully.

Here it is possible to imagine that Simon is better able to deal with the disappointment of having a broken helicopter because of the achievement of being able to say the words to describe the situation. It is as if—as we ourselves know from adult life— often talking about something will take the heat out of the situation. Having the words provides a little more feeling of control over the emotions, and that is true even for toddlers who are only just beginning to use language. Even quite young toddlers who have only a few words will pick up their parents' expressions and hand gestures when something has not gone quite right, saying perhaps "oh dear" or "uh-oh" or "gone" (with hands out, looking questioning), as if such experience are easier to deal with if they can use their parents' mode of dealing with them.

We can see from all of this how quickly children learn and pick up language from their parents by copying them and by absorbing their parents' mode of communication. Not only do these young children mimic their parents naming of objects and naming of feelings and internal states, they increasingly also internalize their parents' understanding of those states as well as their parents' particular style of voicing commands and prohibitions.

> Anna (2 years 3 months) bent down to look at a red berry lying on the ground. The toddler assistant bent down to join her and stretched out to pick it up. Anna said very forcefully, "Don't touch!"

By the time your child is into his third year his vocabulary will have increased considerably, and he may even be beginning to speak in short sentences and to ask questions. He will increasingly be able to use language to help him identify with aspects of mother or father in their absence, and this will give him a way to begin to have more control over his emotions and to substitute words for action at times when the action might get him into trouble.

We shall see in chapter 7 how language helps the older toddler prepare for communication with the wider world—with peers and adults other than those in his immediate family.

Difficulties with language

There is a huge variation in the speed at which different children learn to speak. Their cognitive capacities mature at different rates. Their innate constitutional characteristics and also the familial environment within which they begin to experiment with communication vary greatly. There is much controversy about how children learn to speak—about whether, for example, the capacity to speak grammatically is an innate or learned characteristic—which is beyond the scope of this book. However, whatever the fundamental origins of the development of language are, it is clear that the emotional context in which it arises is critically important.

If, for example, a toddler has been denied the earliest experiences of having his wishes gratified, he will not have the motivation or expectation that he can have wishes fulfilled and so the impetus to communicate his wants will be absent. How can one vocalize a wish for something of which one has no experience? In this way early deprivation will hamper language development. On the other hand, too much premature fulfilment of wishes for the toddler will also interfere with the development of language. If mother is always available with the feed, or always knows what the toddler is saying before he has even had a chance to try to communicate, then, once again, the motivation for the toddler to experiment with vocalization does not arise.

It is clear that a degree of separation between parent and toddler, combined with the parent's emotional availability from a little more of a distance than was the case in the child's first year, are essential for the child to begin to use his voice to communicate. Such subtle calibrations of emotional distance might seem like a tall order, but in fact most parents and toddlers achieve that instinctively. For some, though, it is harder. Their child may have been ill during his first year, and his parents may feel more protective about him, finding it difficult not to pre-empt his every wish. Sometimes, even though the toddler himself has not been unwell, the parents' experience of another child or of a previous stillbirth or miscarriage will mean that they are more protective of the toddler, and they will find it harder than some to allow him the necessary degree of a sense of agency to move him as quickly as others to begin to vocalize. Sometimes the parents' own current or past emotional experiences have an impact on their child's capacity to use language effectively:

> Meme's mother was a single-parent refugee from a war-torn country on the other side of the world, and her own family remained there. Like many parents in a similar position, she felt very strongly that she wanted her daughter to speak her own language as her mother tongue. She spoke exclusively to her in her native language and did not translate or mediate on her behalf when with English speakers. She missed her own family hugely and longed for the time when she could return to her country. Meme learnt to speak her mother's language, but she had a very exclusive relationship with her, becoming clingy and controlling. She could not speak any English and looked perplexed when she saw her mother speaking to others in English. Gradually she began to understand English during her third year, but she did not speak any by the time she started nursery school, and she remained a child who had a great deal of difficulty separating from her mother.

Here we can see how language development and emotional development intertwine. For this mother, isolated and lonely in this country, and separated from her own family of origin, it was very important to keep her daughter close—understandably, it was as if her daughter was fated to become a substitute link to her own family, using language as the link. As she adapts to English life and school, Meme will certainly become bilingual and will probably continue to speak to her mother exclusively in her mother's language of origin. However, the role her mother's language has played in her development has, to some extent, also determined the nature of their relationship, and it will have an impact on the way Meme will deal with her feelings about other relationships in the future.

In this way, language is forged out of an emotional relationship, but language also shapes the emotional relationship:

Mary was an extremely bright, precocious little girl whose mother had suffered from postnatal depression during her first six months. She learnt to speak early. A somewhat anxious child, she was quite vigilant of her mother and seemed to be very aware of her moods, finding it difficult to play away from her despite her tremendous curiosity about the world. By the time she was 2 years old, she was beginning to develop a stutter. It was as if her thoughts were going too fast for her ability to express them. Her parents became very worried about this, as well as about the impact of mother's postnatal depression on her development, and they responded with giving her a lot of anxious attention. With some reassurance from the GP, they became a little more relaxed and she, too, then relaxed more, and the stutter improved. However, after the birth of a baby sister, Mary's stutter returned, along with crying tantrums and an inability to leave mother's side. The mother was helped to recognize that the extent of her own guilt and her tremendous wish to protect Mary from the impact of the birth of her sister might be related to the mother's own feelings as a child of huge resentment and jealousy after the birth of her own baby brother. She began to see that her own conflict over resentment of Mary's demands yet wishing to protect her stemmed from her own childhood and made it hard for her to stay firm yet sympathetic in the face of Mary's emotional roller-coaster. Instead, she was being drawn in to giving Mary more and more anxious attention when she stuttered. A one-off visit to the speech therapist reassured both parents as well as giving them some hints about how to respond to their daughter's communications. They relaxed more about Mary's resilience and could allow themselves to be firmer with her, and as a result she became more resilient. The stutter disappeared gradually.

Some toddlers do develop speech impairments as they learn to talk. Sometimes these are organically caused, and other times they are more emotionally related. Often the cause is a mixture of the two. If you find yourself becoming anxious about this, it is probably helpful to look for some outside help; otherwise, it is likely that your anxiety will be picked up by the toddler and will make the situation worse. Talking over the problem with your GP can provide some reassurance, as can a referral to a speech therapist. Usually at this age it is not a serious problem and will pass as the child becomes more fluent and as you become more relaxed.

whose body is it anyway?

Pleasures

The toddler years are characterized by a huge shift in the child's relationship to his body, accompanied by much physical activity and exploration. We have seen in chapter 1 how the very young toddler can become utterly absorbed and fascinated by what he can achieve physically. He is propelled by curiosity about both his own and others' bodies, watching, touching, smelling, and tasting. Such exploration allows him to develop a sense of his own body's coherence and autonomy, integral to his growing sense of his own identity.

An important part of this development is his capacity to experience sensual feelings. As a baby, his early feeds and general caretaking will have been accompanied by sensations of intensely pleasurable physical satisfaction. To begin with, he will not have been able to identify the distinction between his own and his mother's body as the source of satisfaction, but as time goes on he will associate those pleasurable sensations with the presence of someone caring for him. As he becomes more physically competent, he will start to explore both her body as well as his own, and in his own body he will find areas and activities that will give him intense pleasure. Sometimes these activities will be recreating the pleasurable sensations he had experienced when being cared for by mother, such as fondling his own hair or stroking his earlobe gently or sucking his thumb, for example, but others are ones he discovers on his own. He may have enjoyed genital sensations during nappy changes and may also touch and play with his genitals as part of his own exploration, finding the experience pleasurable. It is an important aspect of your toddler's developing sense of pride and confidence that he discovers that his body can be a source of pleasure. He is learning what is his and what is yours. It is good that he can begin to learn that what-is-his and what what-is-his does can be sources of pleasure and that he can derive pride and confidence both from his body and from its functions.

Your toddler, then, is in the throes of learning that it is his body and that he exists in it. At the same time, he is not yet entirely master of it and does not want to lose the pleasure of his parents' care of it. The struggle between the toddler's wish for autonomy and his wish for dependency becomes easily focused on his body. Added to this mix are our (and society's) expectations that our toddler should be beginning to be able to have some control of his bodily functions by the time he is over 3 years old.

As your toddler moves towards his third birthday, you will probably have expectations and wishes about him being able to take more care of himself without your help. People differ greatly in just how quickly they want their child to become more independent, but most will be hoping that their child is showing signs of moving towards being able to feed himself (even if only with his fingers or a spoon) and drink from a beaker, be showing signs of being potty-trained (if not already being there), be able to go to sleep on his own, and be beginning to be able to put some of his clothes on by himself. All of these developments concern his ability to begin to take responsibility for his body. However, for many parents and toddlers this gradual progression from the complete dependence of babyhood to more autonomy is no easy ride, and often the toddler's body becomes the place where the battles are fought out.

What goes in

In the first few months of life, it is likely that your child's relationship with you centred round his feeds. You and he got to know each other through the way you each responded to cues from the other in the context of his appetite. If he cried, it is likely that you would assume first that he was hungry and would feed him. Your feeds, whether breast or bottle, will have given you a much-valued opportunity to provide for him. To be able to quieten a baby through giving nourishment is, for most parents, a source of much pleasure. And for him, the moments of alertness while being fed will also have been moments when he would have taken in all sorts of other experiences— of being comforted, secure, close, and also stimulated—experiencing through all his senses far more than just the satiation of hunger.

It will not always have gone right and may have been a source of anxiety and upset as well. It will have been affected by the baby's innate constitution, state of health, and position in the family and by his parents' emotional state. But there is no doubt that, for both parent and child, feeding will have been an important shared emotional experience. It is not surprising, then, that moving away from that shared intensity of feeding can sometimes be hard for both parents and child. For some parents, though, it can be a huge relief to have a child who is more able to be independent.

Probably by the time your baby reaches his first birthday you will have introduced solid foods to him, and he may be beginning to feed himself finger foods or with a spoon. There will have been other changes too—now he no longer lies in your arms for feeds but sits up and, while he is feeding, takes an active interest not just in your face but in the world around him. Others can feed him more easily now, too: fathers and siblings. And he can take more control of what goes in by averting his head from the spoon or even by throwing the food on the floor. In fact, this could easily be your first experience of your child expressing his opinions about something independently of your own views.

Battles over feeding

Suddenly parents can find themselves feeling very controlled by this little creature, so recently a passive baby, now able to take the initiative over what he eats and does not eat. Parents can very quickly feel that their only-just-a-toddler has them over a barrel. He refuses to eat what is good for him. He shuts his mouth or turns his head against what the parents feel is the nourishment that will keep him alive. Their toddler has a strong weapon indeed if his parents dig their heels in, determined in their anxiety to "make" him eat what they think he ought to. In fact, if it develops into a battle, it is one that only the toddler can win. Short of pushing the food forcibly down his throat, no parent can make a child eat what he does not want. And one of the most important lessons for parents of toddlers is to be selective about the fights they want with their child, making sure they do not pick ones that they cannot win.

At this stage, it is important to remember that it is most unlikely that your toddler will willingly starve himself. It is likely that he is, instead, enjoying the opportunity to have a bit of control over his destiny, just as he is beginning to enjoy more control over his increasingly independent mobility. It is possible that, from his point of view, in this arena—as in others during this phase—he is being given somewhat mixed messages. He is being encouraged to feed himself, to use his fingers, to grab hold of the spoon, and so on, and yet he seems to displease the adults when he really seriously takes control.

It is certainly not convenient or pleasant if your toddler takes it into his head to refuse his food, to play with it, or to throw it around, but it is important not to see this as delinquent wilful naughtiness on his part. The more relaxed you can be about it, and the more you can allow him to experiment over control of his intake and enjoy the process, the better. This may be difficult, particularly for parents who themselves have issues with eating or with matters of control:

Maria's father had given up work to stay at home to look after her. He wanted to make sure Maria (2 years) ate food that was good for her. She would refuse and get down from her chair. He would follow her around, forcing "healthy" fruit into her mouth. She became more obstinate and contrary, and they would argue over it. Later she would surreptitiously eat other food when he was not looking. Once her father became a little more aware of his own feelings about his loss of control through his work and his sense of victimization in his own family background, he began to relax more with Maria and relinquish some of his compulsion to control her food.

If you find yourself getting into battles over feeding, it is probably important to step back a bit and to take time to think about why it is happening. If your toddler seems to want more control over what he eats, can you offer him some choice? You may not want him to eat junk food or sweet things, but there is a range of foods that are healthy. He might like to choose between raisins, grapes, and a banana. He might like to be offered a cracker instead of bread fingers. Sometimes toddlers prefer to eat on their own. At other times they may want to join in the social life at mealtimes. It is important that together you find a way of managing meal times that works for you. If he is a messy eater, you can take precautions by putting a plastic

sheet around where he eats—even on the floor if necessary—
to make his behaviour a little more tolerable to you. It is
important to remember that, unbelievable and interminable
though it may seem, he will gradually learn to eat in a more
socially acceptable fashion. And he will also learn to eat foods
that are good for him and learn to read the messages of his own
hunger—as long as it does not become an issue for the two of
you that has roots that are nothing to do with his appetite.

During her pregnancy with Peter, his mother had nursed her
own mother through the final stages of a terminal illness. His
maternal grandmother died a few weeks after his birth, and
his mother was bereft. Shortly afterwards, Peter was hospital-
ized for a severe tummy bug. Already a small baby, when he
was discharged he had lost some weight, but the doctors were
not overly concerned. Despite reassurances from her GP and
health visitor, his mother became very preoccupied with Peter's feeding habits and was anxious that he was not eating
enough. She spent hours trying to persuade him to take his
milk, and there was barely a minute between the feeds as they
took so long. He remained a slight little boy, rather delicate
looking and anxious. When he was 2 years old, he was hospi-
talized again for a mild infection and lost his appetite. His
mother's anxieties about his weight again resurfaced. Shortly
after, when he was feeling better, one mealtime he started
stuffing grapes into his mother's mouth. She turned her head
away, telling him to stop as she did not like it, but he persisted.
It was only when she realized the connection between what he
was doing and her own anxious force-feeding of him when he
was a baby and more recently when he was ill that she was
able to relax a little and allow him more choice about when
and what to eat.

Here we can see how despite this mother's best intentions, circumstances combined to make it hard for her to give her son
the autonomy he needed in order to learn the messages of his

appetite. It is possible that his mother, so recently grieving for her own mother's death, at some level worried that her son might also fade away if he did not put on more weight. It is also possible that her own wishes for a mother to comfort her in her distress were attributed to her son. Confusing her own "hungry" needs with his, perhaps, she was unable to put him down when he no longer wanted feeding, and feeling emotionally empty herself she may have felt that food was the only comfort she could give him.

Weaning a toddler off the breast or bottle can also be difficult for some parents. Many want to continue as long as they possibly can. They enjoy the moments of peace and the feeling of togetherness that comes with feeding a baby, albeit a growing one, in their arms. It may be the only time of day when they can completely relax with their child. For others, it is a quick and easy way to provide comfort. There is none of the effort of having to distract them while preparing other food. For other parents, the prospect of the pain of separation and anticipated sense of deprivation that they imagine their baby will feel is activated by their own experiences of pain at separation or their own sense of deprivation stemming from their own childhood:

Chris's mother felt ashamed of breastfeeding Chris when he was 2 years 11 months but found it very difficult to stop. She tried distracting him with biscuits, but he would take the biscuits and still force himself onto her lap and push up her blouse for a feed. A depressed single parent from a significantly deprived background, she found that the feeds were comforting her, despite her shame. She found it hard to resist her child's forceful demands and could not bring herself to say "no", especially at times of transition—when they were about to leave the nursery, for example. Once she was helped to understand how her own feelings were interfering with the way she interacted with Chris over his feeds, she began to find it easier to find alternative ways to distract him from his hunger.

Another mother recently moved from abroad and, feeling isolated from her own family of origin, found that her daughter, Theresa (3 years), was getting bad nappy rash from her constantly soaking nappies. Theresa could not be weaned off a constant supply of bottles of apple juice, which she sucked at almost like a dummy. Once mother acknowledged how much she missed her own mother and how lonely she felt within her marriage, she began to be able to separate more her own feelings of need for comfort from Theresa's. She gradually began to replace the apple juice with water, and Theresa slowly began to lose interest in the bottle.

Parents vary a lot in their opinions about when it is appropriate for their baby or toddler to give up the breast or bottle. For some it cannot come quickly enough, whereas others believe it should be carried on as long as possible, looking to other cultures for confirmation of their views. Sometimes babies and toddlers make it clear themselves when they are ready to give up, but sometimes it is harder for them to renounce an easy and pleasurable way to find soothing comfort at times of distress. For this reason, parents cannot rely entirely on the messages their child gives them about wanting to stop, and they may find they need to make the decision on behalf of their child as well as themselves. If you are one of those parents who want to continue as long as possible, it is nevertheless worth giving some thought to whether your toddler may be getting mixed messages about how grown-up you want him to be. Are you expecting him to be potty-trained, playing with other children, and ready for nursery school while simultaneously giving him messages that he is still a babe-in-arms? It might be confusing for him.

As with many of the hiccups in bringing up your toddler, if you find things are not going as smoothly as you had hoped or you feel that, for example, your attempt to wean is becoming emotionally charged, it is often helpful to remember that your child has not one but two parents. Even if you are a single parent with no contact with the other parent, it is likely that you have other people in your life who could help out. Often another parent or close friend will see things from a slightly different perspective, and the intensity of the emotions between you and your child that have developed will be lessened in the company of the other. The child may find it much easier to allow himself to be weaned if father is more emotionally available at the time (see also chapter 6), and particularly if you have worked out a joint strategy between you.

What comes out: potty training

For many first-time parents, the prospect of their child learning to control his bladder and his bowels seems as remote as a miracle. They cannot imagine how it happens. And as their baby develops into a strong-willed 2-year-old toddler, with tantrums brimming over whenever his wishes are thwarted, the task of "getting him" to use a potty—let alone a toilet—seems increasingly remote. When pre-school nursery looms with a condition of entry that their child is "dry", panic really begins to set in. How does potty training indeed happen?

As we know, children develop physically at very different rates, and this is reflected in the variety of ages when ordinary healthy children learn, for example, to crawl or to walk. In the same way, it is important to recognize that individual toddlers develop the physical control over their anal and urethral sphincter muscles at very different ages. Such control occurs only when the child has upright mobility, and it is usually not physically secure until the child has been walking for at least three or four months.

For children to be able to take control of peeing and pooing, they must also be able to recognize their own bodily sensations, to remember previous similar experiences, and to be able to anticipate the actions required to deal with them. It is helpful, too, if the parents can recognize a pattern in the child and help him to begin to recognize his own bodily patterns.

If only it were simply a matter of physical capacities, though. The not uncommon response of panic in parents, described above, betrays the fact that for all of us there is a primitive emotional component to potty training.

It is likely that when your child was a baby, before he started eating solid food, and especially if you were breastfeeding him, you were surprised not to be more disgusted with having to deal with his bodily waste products. Although not always particularly pleasurable, cleaning him up after he had soaked his nappy or pooed is something that parents of a newborn cope with reasonably happily and accept as part of the package that comes with caring for their baby. And, in fact, for many parents the physical closeness and intimacy of caring for their child's body, over and above feeding him, can be very enjoyable. Babies are often more alert and playful at times when they are being cleaned up and changed, and it is often a time when they begin to relate to the wider environment more than when they are feeding.

However, it is likely that as your baby grows bigger and as his diet changes, you will find that your attitude to his waste products begins to undergo a shift. More often the smells become unpleasant, the volume is bigger, and the pleasure of cleaning up begins to wane. He is alert all the time now, sometimes so much so that changing him is a much more difficult job as he refuses to cooperate and wants to carry on with whatever he was doing. There will be more of a contrast in your attitude to his body when it is dirty or wet and when it is clean. It is likely that some of your dislike of his smells or of his mess and your delight when he is all cleaned up will be betrayed in your attitude towards him. "That's a big smelly poo", for example, will be followed by "now you're all nice and clean". It may not be as direct as that, but repeated subtle comments of this kind will mean that he will inevitably slowly pick up on the fact that adults do not find smelly or soaking nappies particularly pleasant.

Life with a toddler is messy in all sorts of ways. To many parents it can seem as if everything is spilling out all over the place. He dribbles saliva and drips snot, he spills his food and smears it on your and his clothes and chairs. Toys seem to get everywhere: the contents of the boxes and drawers he has been investigating, the pieces of paper that he has chewed or torn up, water, food. It can feel as if you are drowning in mess—that nowhere manages to escape the debris that he leaves in his wake. It can easily feel as if the mess will stay forever. Emotions, too, can feel as if they are rather raw and messy, spilling out in ways that feel much less controlled than in the days before he was born. As we have said, toddler passions can be intense and overwhelming for the toddler, but they may also evoke equally intense and overwhelming emotions in his parents. We may be surprised how we respond with our own toddler-like passions, and we sometimes have to face a tremendous urge in ourselves to respond in kind, with our own mess, or our own wish to make a mess. At other times, our reaction may be to become the complete opposite: tremendously controlled and controlling, not allowing any mess anywhere, and cleaning up the house so thoroughly that there is no time for playing with our child.

As he gets older your toddler will show in many ways that he wants to be like the bigger people in his life—his older siblings and his parents—and he will want to copy them. He will also, a lot of the time, when his more primitive urges for immediate gratification do not conflict too much, want to please those he loves. In this way he will pick up on your wishes for him to be a "big" boy, more in control of his bladder and bowels, more able sometimes, even, to enjoy helping you tidy up after him.

At the same time, often during his second year you will find him utterly absorbed by play that involves messing, and its opposite, controlling the mess. Toddlers around the age of 2 years usually love, for example, water play. They will spend prolonged periods of concentration catching water from a dripping tap in containers and then pouring the water from one container to another. They may enjoy the consistency of Play-Doh, pushing and pulling it and mixing up all the colours, and then using it to cut shapes or watch you cutting shapes out of it. They also enjoy stuffing or hammering toys and shapes into holes and watching them come through the other side.

Simultaneously, as their muscles and nerves mature, it is possible that you will notice that your toddler is becoming much more aware of the internal functions of his body. He may pause in his activities when he pees or poos, suddenly distracted and perhaps puzzled by the sensation. If you have always been open with him and talked with him about his body and what it does, it will be much easier and less worrying for him when he begins to have these sensations. You will no doubt have your own language to describe it, but whatever you use it is important that he knows that he is only doing and experiencing what everyone else does. He may well be interested in the bathroom and toilet, and at this stage you could introduce him to the potty or the toddler toilet-seat and step—whatever arrangements you think would be best for you and him. He needs help in knowing that you anticipate that one day he will be able to manage his body himself and that, for example, the potty is going to be a way to help him do that.

Once it has been established that the potty is a friendly, non-threatening object that will help him become the big boy who can take charge of his body and who, in part of his mind, he would like to be, you may find that the toddler "by myself" urge kicks in and he volunteers to try to use it one day completely out of the blue. Most toddlers, though, will need some prompting from their parents, and it can be helpful to give this a bit of forward planning. It is important that you engage the toddler's wish for independence, as well as support his investment in his own body and his wish to please you. If you choose a time to start potty training him when you are preoccupied and when he is likely to be more needy and to regress to more babyish feelings—for example, around the time of pregnancy and the birth of a sibling, when he is about to start nursery, when there is illness or a death in the family, when you are moving house— you may be setting him up to fail. At times like those, the last thing he will want is to feel more grown-up; indeed, if he has already been potty-trained, it is very common to relapse for a while.

Instead, choose a period that is convenient to you, when you will have time to praise him for his efforts and support him through the inevitable accidents on the path to success. Make sure you can make practical arrangements that make it easier for you and him. Does he prefer a potty or to use a toddler toilet-seat? Can you let him run around in the summer with no nappy on so he can see what happens when he pees and poos? Often, people find it easier to potty train their toddlers in the summer.

Difficulties and accidents

For most toddlers, it will not be an entirely straightforward process, and there will be accidents, which the toddler may well experience as humiliating. There he was, thinking he could be a big boy in control of everything he wishes, and instead he feels like a baby betrayed by his body. However much of a nuisance and disappointment it is to you, it is important to treat these accidents sensitively and to reinforce your expectation that he will get there one day but that there will inevitably be hiccups on the way. Sometimes the timing is wrong—perhaps he is not yet old enough to manage what is being expected of him or he is not yet motivated enough. If, after a few days, you feel that the pain—his and yours—of the accidents is outweighing the pleasure of achievement, then it may be sensible to give up for a few weeks and try again a little later.

Sometimes children of this age develop elaborate and frightening fantasies about what comes out of their bodies. In their minds, their poo may take on a life of its own, which means the child can be very frightened to see it lurking in the potty. At other times, the fantasies may be about how precious and valuable the poo is and how, therefore, it must be preserved inside the body.

It can be difficult for parents to maintain and convey to their toddler the low-key level of expectation that their toddler will do it on his own. It is easy to feel exasperated in the presence of an almost 3-year-old who apparently wilfully and knowingly withholds his poo, hiding in a corner perhaps and refusing to use the potty. There is a risk that potty training can get caught up in a conflict over ownership of the destiny of the body and its waste. Your toddler may start to feel that you are so invested in his success in being "clean" that it is no longer his responsibility. And he may respond with a demonstration of his wish that it be his and his alone, not even wanting to share the production of his waste. He will behave how he wants over matters to do with his body and his poo by withholding. At the same time, it is likely that he will be a bit ashamed of what he is doing, knowing it will displease you, and he will hide. Very soon it becomes a conflict with you and your wishes, rather than something you have to help him struggle with in his body. It is easy for the toddler's developmentally normal appropriate wish for control over the bodily urges to be sidelined into the equally normal—but not very helpful, in this instance—battle for control with parents. As with feeding and eating, the task in hand becomes hijacked by other emotional agendas, and the bodily processes are hijacked by misleading messages.

At times like this it is important to take a step back and think about how to defuse the situation. Are you asking him to do more than he is capable of, are there reasons why he might be frightened of his poo, is he going through a phase when he is particularly angry with you for some other reason? It may help to talk to him about what he might be feeling and to convey to him the sense that you know it is up to him to decide when he is ready. It is important to defuse the conflict with you and to help him take back the responsibility for being clean.

For a minority of children, mostly boys, there may be a continuing difficulty in being fully continent by the time they start nursery, or even primary school. Wetting accidents during the day and bedwetting at night are not uncommon at this age. If this is the case with your child, remember—hard though it may be at the time—that he cannot help it and that you are not alone with this problem. If, though, you are worried, you might like some professional help. A visit to your GP is probably the best starting-point. It is important, however, in your discussions to keep in mind the need to be sensitive to your child's feelings and to be aware how easily humiliated he is likely to feel about not being grown-up enough to control his body as he is expected to do.

separations, sleeping, and sibling rivalry

Sleeping and separations

The toddler years are dominated by a gradual process of separation between the child and his parents. We have seen how the struggles over the pull back towards dependence and babyhood and the push forward towards independence dominate the toddler's (and the parents'!) development in all spheres. Both he and you—his parents—wish for more autonomy, and yet despite this wish, you at times also long for more togetherness and closeness. Negotiating the way between these opposing pulls is one of the most important tasks of these years.

As with feeding, weaning, and potty training, which were the topics of our previous chapter, managing sleeping and separations are at base to do with allowing and encouraging more bodily autonomy in your toddler. And difficulties, particularly with feeding and weaning, often overlap into difficulties with sleeping and separations.

The mother of Steve (2 years 6 months) felt permanently exhausted as well as worried by his interrupted sleep and inability to move out of the parental bed. To her shame, she was still breastfeeding Steve at night to make him go to sleep. She was also worried that Steve was very clingy, demanding her attention constantly, and refusing to let anyone else take care of him. She wanted him to start nursery when he was 3 years old and could not see how he was going to be able to part from her.

During the course of work with Steve's mother, it emerged that her own parents had separated when she was very little and that as an adult she was estranged from her own mother, whom she found intensely difficult, needy, and unsupportive. It also became clear that Steve's father was extremely busy as well as travelling abroad for long periods of time with his work. Although, at one level, mother was tormented by Steve's wakefulness and clinginess and did everything in her power to combat it, it also seemed possible that, despite her best intentions, she was conflicted about the extent to which she wanted Steve to move away from her. It was likely that, at another level, she was comforted by Steve's need of her and by his presence in her bed, in the absence of father. And it was possible that she was also trying to be a very different mother to Steve from the way she felt her own mother had been (and continued to be) to her. It was only when some of her feelings about her marriage, her sense of isolation, and her relationship to her own parents were brought into the open that she was able to turn towards her husband to enlist his support both in being firm with Steve about the need for him to sleep in his own bed and to help Steve begin to find his own ways to soothe himself ready for sleep, as an alternative to breast-feeding. This took time, but gradually as Steve appeared to begin to understand that there were limits to the extent to which he could control his mother, he became less demanding of her and more accepting of others, began to sleep in his own bed, and gave up the breast.

Of course, toddler sleeping problems are very common, and not all can so easily be attributed to parental need for the comfort of a baby. But, nevertheless, there is frequently some guilt on the part of parents about putting their child down to sleep and allowing themselves time to get on with their own lives, separately from their child. It is as if sometimes parents feel that they are abandoning their toddler, when they say goodnight to him, to a terrifying fate. And sometimes this struggle is about coming to terms with the presence of a third person in a relationship.

Coming to terms with threesomes

Threesomes are much harder to maintain than twosomes. With three, there is a fear that one will feel left out, excluded by the other two. And those feelings of being excluded are most often attributed to the toddler in the threesome, easily identified as vulnerable and needy. French psychoanalysts refer to the role of the mother of the day—maternal, caring for the child—and the mother of the night—a woman in a sexual relationship with the father of the child. It is as if all three—mother, father, and toddler—have to come to terms with the reality of generational and sexual difference in being able to allow the toddler to sleep at night in his own bed, and sometimes this is quite an adjustment to make. Even with single parents where there is no father present, it is important for mother to make clear that there is a third presence in her life, an "other" from her toddler, whether it is a new partner, fantasies of one, or other family or good friends from her own generation.

Learning that his parents have private time and space that is not readily accessible to him will help your toddler in his struggles to become more independent. Acknowledging your wish for privacy may also help him learn, when he is older, about his own appropriate need for privacy. It may also help him to develop a sense of his right for protection from over-intrusive involvement: that he has private parts of his body and that his wish to have his private space or time should be respected.

Leaving: your toddler's feelings

You may by now be protesting that toddlers are vulnerable and needy and that they cannot cope with being abandoned by their parents to sleep in their own beds at night or even to tolerate a babysitter so their parents can have a bit of a life of their own. It is true that it takes time for babies and toddlers to learn that when their parents disappear, they have not gone for ever. As mentioned in chapter 1, by the time of their first birthday our toddlers have for several months been able to distinguish between those significant people who comfort them, mainly their parents and close family, and those who are much less familiar. As we have seen (chapter 1), fear in the presence of unfamiliar faces reaches its peak towards the end of the first year, when you may notice your child finding it particularly hard to settle with anyone else. This can come as a surprise to parents who have had a very sociable baby, and they can suddenly start worrying that their child is going to be forever insecure and clingy. It can be helpful to remember that this is an ordinary phase and its intensity will pass—although, of course, for all of us, transitions from familiar people and situations remain times of increased emotional vulnerability.

Some toddlers are by nature more timid and less receptive to new experiences than others, and this will have an impact on their subsequent development. Some children seem to be born constitutionally more emotionally robust than others. Other toddlers may have been affected by their very early relation-ships with their parents—often in ways that are unavoidable—to the extent that these toddlers feel in the grip of complete inconsolable panic when they cannot see their familiar care-givers. Such children will find it harder to grow out of the phase of stranger-anxiety and may remain intensely demanding of their parents' attention; alternatively, and paradoxically, they may respond with an attitude of almost premature independence from their parents, as if they have given up on them being available to comfort them.

Parents of such toddlers may have a harder time helping their child adjust to the need to learn to go to sleep alone and to learn that separations will be followed in good time by reunions. But at some time, though, all parents have to deal with a toddler who is upset at being parted from familiar faces, whether it is at bedtime or when the toddler is left with a babysitter. When this happens, it is helpful to try to understand what might be going through the toddler's mind, even though it is most unlikely he will be able to tell you. Is it behaviour that is unusual for his character, might there be some external explanation for it, is it part of a normal phase of development, has he started to have nightmares that he is frightened of, has he had a day when he has been particularly cross with you, are you preoccupied and worried by anything unusual, has his routine been upset in any way? Thinking about these sorts of issues may help you find a way to respond with appropriate reassurance and with physical comfort if necessary. Sometimes, if you are aware that he is especially distressed by partings, it can be helpful to play out some hide-and-seek or peek-a-boo games so that, through play, he can master his feelings of helplessness in the face of a loss. Like many other things in life, children have to learn about separations. They have to learn that goodbyes are followed by returns, that unavailability for a time is followed by availability on a reasonably predictable basis.

Some children can be helped through the periods of absence with the presence of the special toys or pieces of blanket or bits of fluff that some babies and toddlers develop a strong attachment to. These "transitional objects", as they are sometimes called, may have a particular texture or smell that reminds the child of the parent and gives comfort to the child in her absence. They provide a sort of pathway for the child to access the sense of the presence of the love of the parent in her absence. For our toddlers who are still struggling to remember familiar faces when they are away or even loving ones when crises are happening, to have a reminder of earlier feelings of loving care—perhaps associated with being fed or cuddled as a baby—will allow them to tolerate being on their own. You will find that the particular object selected is invested with intense pleasure and becomes critically important for the toddler, who may well be inconsolable if it is lost or washed or changes its texture. This is because at moments when he feels alone, to him the "blanket", with all its familiar characteristics, is so closely associated with his mother's love that it almost becomes that love.

Leaving: your feelings

If you feel that your toddler's difficulties are neither explicable by the phase he is going through nor the result of a particularly difficult period of emotional turmoil, but are more to do with a more pervasive pattern of difficulty with regulating his emotions enough to fall asleep on his own, then you have to decide whether or not it is something you wish to change. There is a view that just as in those other cultures where children share their parents' bed, so too our children would benefit from sleeping with their parents until well beyond toddlerhood. Some believe that giving in to the toddler's wishes in this way will make him feel more secure and contented. However, there is a risk that your child may experience your indulgence of him in your bed as evidence of your inability to resist his controlling urges, as evidence that he, rather than you, is the one in control and that he has to look after you with your anxious wish to please and placate him rather than to stand up to him.

Surprising though it may seem, questions of just who is looking after whom and who needs whom are often relevant in these situations. The feelings evoked in a parent by a persistently crying toddler are often overwhelming. Sometimes the pain at having to deal with the situation on one's own, and our toddler's pain can be hard to distinguish. As with feeding and weaning difficulties, it is often helpful to turn to your partner or a friend for an ally, almost as someone to look after you in your upset at having to deal with your toddler.

For us as parents, there are many reasons why it is hard to resist our toddlers' distress when we separate from them, and our feelings can complicate our capacity to think about and respond to the situation appropriately. As we have seen, Steve's mother's own sense of isolation made her turn—in ways of which she was completely unaware, and despite her overt intentions—to Steve to comfort herself, making it hard for mother and toddler to part from each other.

It does not always take such an intense experience for things to go slightly askew. Often mothers are understandably ambivalent about the way their growing child is interfering in their lives, and they may desperately want to protect him from their negative feelings. They may instead, almost by way of compensation, respond to what they feel are such unacceptable feelings by becoming overprotective.

Such mixed feelings can become particularly intense in the middle of the night, when parents are understandably angry at having their sleep interrupted. To many, the thought of such strong hostility towards such a tiny being is so unacceptable that parents may respond by being particularly concerned, fearful that putting the baby down again will commit it to the mercy of their hostile feelings. Other parents may find it difficult to accept that their toddler is expressing a difference of opinion from them, often for the first time. They may be unhappy that their offspring sees things differently from them, feeling that agreement is essential. In fact, though, there is a risk that the toddler will then have a sense that mixed feelings or angry protest cannot be tolerated and that separate views cannot be permitted.

Bedtimes and night-times, when parents and toddlers are tired, are times when such conflictual feelings are at their most intense, and it is hardly surprising that these moments become problematic. As we have seen, toddlers are extremely perceptive. Their antennae are on the alert much of the time, their curiosity feeding the dramatic pace of absorption of knowledge about themselves and the world. They will inevitably pick up on parental anxiety and, as a result, risk becoming more rather than less anxious themselves when exposed to it. Such mutual responses can quickly turn into a downward cycle of further anxiety in the parents, followed by further upset and anxiety in the child. What parents hope to achieve with their presence brings out in these circumstances the very opposite: greater worry and panic in the child. It is usually, in fact, more helpful to have the courage and confidence to convey to your child that he will learn to sleep on his own, protecting him from experiencing your anxiety and helping him to feel safe in your faith at his capacity to do so by being both understanding of his predicament and also firm about bedtimes and night-time waking.

It is important to keep in mind, as with feeding and potty training, that he will benefit most from your quiet understanding, coupled with unpersecuting assurance that he will get there in the end and the confidence in him to do so that allows you to leave him despite his initial howls of protest, rather than hovering over him anxiously, which risks making him more, rather than less, worried himself. Just as your toddler is quick to pick up on your anxious or angry emotions and become more upset by them, so will he be quick to pick up on your quiet assurance that he will be okay and will get to sleep. As with all these milestones, there will be backsliding at times of stress and illness, but conveying a sense of calm knowledge and expectation that having been able to do it before, he will be able to do it again, will reap benefits as your child is less exposed to your very infectious anxiety.

Daytime separations

Much of this chapter so far has been about separations as they affect sleeping problems. What about the child who will not settle with any other adult during the day? Whatever the time of the day at which struggles with separating from your toddler occur, at root the problems, if they are persistent and enduring, are most often based on parental difficulties with having the confidence—and conveying it to their child—that he will be alright in their absence. For some parents, perhaps of a child who has always slept soundly at night, their ambivalence towards their toddler may emerge during the day. They may feel, for example, upset that their toddler is preventing them from resuming a successful career and yet at the same time worried that they are having such unacceptable thoughts about their much-loved child. As with our angry parents of the night-time, such a parent might perhaps become very anxious about her hostility towards her child and compensate by being overprotective when trying to settle him with a nanny or childminder. Again, as with the night-time problems, her anxious guilt is likely to be picked up by the toddler and make him, in turn, more upset than he already was. She will find it hard not to hover on the threshold, wracked with the pain of ambivalence, and she will risk imposing her feelings on the child.

Both you and your child need preparation for these circumstances. You need to feel convinced by your decision to have childcare and assured you have done all the necessary research about what is the best help available. Of course it will not seem as good as your own loving care, but perhaps that is an inevitable part of your decision. You will need, though, to feel as happy as you can with the choice you have made, and your child will need time with you there to get used to the stranger. But having prepared and reassured yourself and him as much as you can, it is very important that you convey to your toddler your confidence that he will survive your absence and may even benefit from it eventually as he learns increasingly to be more independent of you, in these less-than-perfect but more-than-adequate circumstances.

Sibling rivalry

It is understandably a powerful experience for a toddler to have his unique position in the family—whether it is as the firstborn or as the special youngest—usurped by the arrival of a new sibling. We have seen the extent to which the early toddler period is a time when all children are necessarily gradually disabused of their illusions of being the centre of the world. To have a sibling arrive during this time can be a double blow. Here we can see one toddler expressing his ambivalence towards the new arrival:

Jack (1 year 11 months) was playing with the Duplo doll's house. He pushed each little doll forcefully from the house so that it fell onto the floor. He was visibly excited by what he was doing, continuing exuberantly to get rid of the dolls until there was only one left. He was helped to pick all the dolls up and put them back in the house, and then he started throwing them out again, one by one. Again, only one doll was allowed to remain. He repeated the game one more time and then moved over to the prams, where he picked up a large doll and a doll's bottle of "milk". He sat on the carpet with them, opposite his mother who was feeding his newborn baby brother. He supported the doll in one arm, holding the bottle in the other for it to "drink".

Jack expresses his wishes to get rid of all new babies except himself in throwing the dolls out of the house, but then he manages to identify with his mother by joining with her in feeding a baby.

It helps to prepare your toddler for the new arrival, and one way of doing this is to provide opportunities for him to express his feelings about the situation in his play. Some children may not express any anger towards their sibling and may simply take it out on their toys. Others may take it out on their parents by becoming particularly rejecting or testing of one or both. Sometimes the jealousy does not emerge until the baby is quite a bit older and it is clear that the baby is there to stay or is beginning to interfere with the older child's toys and games.

As with separations, the arrival of a sibling brings with it the recognition that the toddler has to share his parent(s) with another. The move from twosomes to triangular relationships brings with it the hard-won recognition for the toddler that he is not the sun around which his planets spin. He has to learn that he is one among others but that being so does not mean that he cannot continue to be loved in his own special way.

As we have seen, anxiety in parents about the impact of the inclusion of another person—or even the introduction of a new interest—into an idealized exclusive twosome is often the cause of difficulties with separating from a toddler. Such concerns about moving from two to three can also complicate relationships following the birth of a sibling and can make it hard for a mother to cope with sibling rivalry. In these circumstances, mother's fear of the eruption of jealousy may make her bend over backwards to protect the older child from any jealousy or hostility towards the younger. Such efforts, of course, are bound to fail, because the reality is that the newborn will take up her time and emotions. Much better is to accept the reality of the situation and help the older child understand that to be no longer in his unique position does not mean that he is no longer loved, and that to be able to share is likely to enhance rather than to diminish the experiences ahead of him. And that the inevitable rivalries and conflicts are not insurmountable but can, instead, be overcome.

Maria (2 years 4 months) was slightly hurt by another child and was crying inconsolably. Mother took her into the garden to play. Meanwhile her 4-month-old baby sister woke and was crying hard for a feed. After ten minutes, Maria continued to insist that mother stay outside to help her on the slide. Mother miserably and weakly gave in to Maria's requests and was unable to move towards her baby. Eventually it was suggested that mother might be able to read to Maria inside while she also fed her baby. They all settled in a corner, with mother reading a book chosen by Maria about fire-engines. After a while, Maria left her mother and went to put the fireman's hat on her head and to play with the toy fire-engine.

Here it is possible to speculate that the mother (who was an oldest sibling herself) became anxious and guilty about her wish to feed her youngest baby and about her anger about Maria's persistent demands. As a result, she was unable to be firm with Maria and allowed Maria to take control. It was only when the family were helped to find a space in which to use their imaginations, in reading the book, that the feelings could become less threatening. They could be shared and expressed in the pretend world of dangerous fires that are mastered by the firemen. And, finally, Maria found the confidence to separate.

7

toddling no more:
the move towards the wider world

In this chapter we look at how the older toddler develops and matures in ways that prepare him for the next phase of his childhood. The seeds of this progress have existed since babyhood and, as we have seen in previous chapters, have been nurtured during his early toddlerhood. But they crystallize into more mature ways of being as the toddler moves much more sturdily into childhood proper.

> On arriving, Sarah (2 years 9 months) appeared unsettled to discover only one other child, a 1-year-old newcomer, in the room. She led her mother over to join him and his mother playing with the Play-Doh. But unusually she did not engage with the activity. She also ignored the newcomers. After some minutes she left them all and went to sit beside the toddler assistant at the doll's house, where she engaged animatedly in a game of posting "letters" through the letter box.
>
> Later, after the arrival of the other children, she, her mother, and the toddler assistant played tea parties, and she distributed cups, saucers "milk", and "sugar" to the others. The newcomer snatched a bowl from her. She looked surprised, but when the toddler assistant explained he is little and did not know about sharing yet, she agreed to let him have it. Soon afterwards, she got in a toy car and said "I'm going for a drive".

In the garden Peter, the same age as Sarah, showed her around what he described as "my house". She drove her car up to the "petrol pump" that Christopher, slightly older and bigger, was using, and grabbed the nozzle from him. He protested, and her mother told her either to wait for her turn or to ask Christopher if she could have the pump. After some hesitation, shyly she asked him if she could have it. He agreed, and after she had used it she passed it back to him. Later, Christopher copied her pushing a doll down the slide. Just before the end of the group, Sarah joined Christopher on the trampoline—he bounced a little less vigorously and made way so she could stand next to him. They jumped joyfully next to one another.

In this picture of one older toddler's typical afternoon, we can see how her newly acquired skills allow her world to open up and how the opening up of her world in turn gives her new experiences and opportunities to further her future development. Being able to share the trampoline effectively, for example, gave her a huge amount of pleasure, allowing her to be braver and more bold in her jumping than before. In many different ways that afternoon, she was learning that in some circumstances two can be more fun than one, that sharing does not always mean deprivation, that sometimes it can bring advantages.

By the time he has reached his third birthday, your toddler will no longer be wobbling as he moves out towards the wider world. The greater security and stability he feels and demonstrates in his body will be paralleled by a firmer sense of himself in relation to others. He will have grown into a much more clearly defined, independent character of his own, more ready and prepared to branch away from his immediate family and to settle with others for longer periods of time. It is with good reason that many nursery schools take children aged 3 years. It is by this age that your toddler is expected to have acquired the self-confidence to relate more or less happily to other adults and to his peers, to have the capacity to delay gratification of his immediate wishes, to tolerate frustration, to play creatively using his imagination, to channel aggression in constructive ways, and to control his bodily functions

However, no 3-year-old will present a perfect picture of these achievements all the time, and many will find most of them elusive for some months to come. Regression to earlier ways of being, especially, but not always, at moments of stress, is entirely normal at all stages of life, and toddlers are no exception. Sarah, for example, needed her mother's presence to help her negotiate her arrival in the playroom when the circumstances were a little unexpected. Equally, an uneven pattern of development, with different aspects of behaviour and social relationships reaching very different levels of maturity within the same child, is entirely normal. Sarah grabs the petrol-pump nozzle from Christopher much as the 1-year-old grabbed the bowl from her. As with previous other developmental milestones, what is most typical is progress that is untidy and uneven and has the appearance of moving one step forward and two steps back.

Tolerating frustration and managing anger

In our vignette of Sarah's afternoon, there is little evidence of the intense passionate ambivalence of the little girl who a few months earlier threw herself on the floor in a tantrum over not getting her wishes. It is Sarah's new-found capacity to tolerate frustration of her wishes and to manage her aggression in, for example, relinquishing her hold on the nozzle in order to ask Christopher's permission, that enables her to move on to a more productive and creative relationship with her peers. The fury of the terrible twos seems to have dissolved. How does this happen?

Although the improvement in physical capacity during toddlerhood is less obvious than during the first year, it is nevertheless extremely significant. We have already considered the impact of becoming vertical rather than horizontal (chapter 1) and of being able to walk and run. But in the third year these capacities consolidate and other new skills are acquired— the toddler has learnt to climb stairs, to run faster, to jump, to build towers of blocks, to post things in boxes, to hammer, to thread, to manipulate small toys, to fold dolls' blankets, and many other feats besides. The cumulative effect of these is that he can now do many tasks on his own. He no longer needs to ask mother for help with them. He can direct himself to where he wants to go and pick up the toys he wants to play with. Sarah easily finds her way between the different activities during the afternoon. She no longer needs her mother's help to find the doll, to get in the car, to go down the slide. The toddler can climb higher than before and feel himself to be as big as or bigger than the grown-ups around him. If he runs away, he has confidence in his ability to run back.

Although there will, of course, be times when he panics and relapses into a need to rush back to his mother when caught in frightening situations, on the whole our toddler's greater physical prowess means that he is no longer so dependent on mother. "By myself" is followed by achievement rather than by a frustrating and humiliating experience of incompetence. And as she appreciates his greater physical power, mother can have increasing confidence in standing back more while he experiments. Her greater confidence in leaving him allows him to feel less trapped and constrained by her constant presence. If, instead, she hovers over him, he will pick up on her worries. The risk will then be that he will in turn become more anxious, feeling unable to branch out and explore because he feels it will leave mother unprotected. As with his progress in all the spheres of his development, it is most helpful to convey the sense of trust and expectation that he will get there in the end, while at the same time creating a safe environment in which the potential for him to succeed is maximized.

These improved physical capacities coincide with important developments in his emotional and cognitive skills. His improved memory means that he can now easily hold objects and people in mind even when they are not present. He can remember where his toys are, and what to expect from familiar situations. Most importantly, though, his memory of his mother and his repeated experiences of reunions with her following separations lessens his need to be vigilant about her presence. We can see how Sarah, following a brief period of needing her mother to get her into the room with new people, can now abandon her freely and then cheerfully join the play leader in a game elsewhere in the room. Later, no longer needing to check on her mother's whereabouts, she joins in games with her peers.

We have seen in previous chapters how such improvements in physical and cognitive skills cannot be considered in isolation from emotional developments. At times of heightened feeling, these newly acquired skills are not always entirely reliable. Memories of pleasant reunions with mother can still be eliminated by feelings of hostility or anxiety, which can lead to panic when she disappears. However, as the toddler grows older such experiences can be mitigated by a growing awareness on his part that it is possible to have mixed feelings about those he loves. Just as he is learning that out of sight is not out of mind, he is also learning that just because Mummy is angry with him now does not mean that she does not also love him. And once aware that love and hate can coexist in others, he can also begin to feel more secure in being able to combine his own loving and hating feelings for those to whom he is close. If a toddler can be helped not to divide the world into all good or all bad, then it will be easier for him to accept that he, too, is not polarized into being utterly good or utterly bad. In this way, it becomes easier for him to believe that his hostile feelings will not drive mother away altogether.

Although, in the example above, Sarah does not talk very much and there is a continuing need for both mother and the play leader to infer from her actions what her thoughts are, to attribute them to her, and to respond to them, extending her understanding a little each time, much as her parents have been doing since she first started to babble, it is clear that at times she is sufficiently able to use language to express her wishes and that this capacity allows her to refrain from enacting them peremptorily. She has the ability, with some help, to negotiate verbally the use of the petrol pump. In this way she is able to share without causing a conflict.

But language development in the third year is important in other respects, too. The use of the personal pronouns "I" and "mine" that generally begins to occur in older toddlers reflects an awareness of the toddler as a subject, as a mind existing in a body, that exists in relation to others, to other minds in other bodies. The awareness that "I am me" by the toddler is a confirmation on his part of an awareness of the separation between the boundaries of his body and mind and the outside world. The move from Sarah identifying herself as "Sarah"— simply imitating what mother calls her—when she first starts to talk about what she is doing, as in "Sarah does it", to "I am driving" reflects her ability to identify herself as a person like other people who also identify and distinguish themselves and their sense of agency in this way.

Boy or girl?

At about the same time as this process of awareness of themselves as a separate person with a sense of agency is emerging, toddlers also begin to develop a sense of the difference between the sexes and of what sex they are. You may notice that your little girl loves to dress up in her mother's necklaces and carries her handbags around wherever she goes. You may find your son wandering around the house carrying his father's hammer. Such identifications will fluctuate, and some children may not experiment with these roles at all. But it is not unusual for toddlers to try out different roles—you will probably find your daughter dressed in glittery shoes on her feet with a fireman's hat on her head, or your son carrying his hammer as he feeds the dolls and pushes them in the buggy. During her short afternoon, Sarah was experimenting with many such adult identifications.

Julia (2 years 6 months) spent the whole afternoon, as in previous weeks, wearing high-heeled silver shoes, carrying a handbag, with a flimsy scarf draped round her shoulders. Very dependent on mother, she found it hard to move from her side. Her mother, who was an ardent feminist and who took no pride in her appearance, never wearing anything other than jeans, a shirt, and flat shoes, was dismayed and puzzled by her daughter's outburst of femininity.

Such stereotypical gender identification alongside experimentation with roles is not unusual in toddlers. Gradually, from about 18 months, your toddler will be building up a much firmer sense of whether he is a boy or a girl, and what that means. The achievement of a sense of one's gender is thought to be determined by the complex integration of biological and psychological factors, very much part of the process of identity building integral to your toddler's development. Biological, anatomical, environmental, and social influences interweave to determine where on the masculine–feminine continuum your toddler positions himself. Although influenced by and usually identical with his anatomical sex, it may not necessarily correspond to it.

It is inevitable that, as parents, our relationship to our own and to the opposite gender will have a distinct impact on our children of the same and of the opposite sex to us. As a parent, your fantasies, expectations, and your own childhood experiences of what it means to be either a boy or a girl will strongly influence the way you handle your child in relation to his gender. As a mother, for example, it is likely that a baby daughter will evoke more powerful feelings of identification—knowing from the inside what it is to be a daughter to a mother—than a baby son would. A daughter might also evoke stronger feelings of rivalry in the mother in relation to the baby's father than a son would. Similarly a father will be more able to identify with a baby boy and will attribute to his daughter characteristics influenced by his earliest and later fantasies about what it means to be female.

In the case above of Julia, we cannot know with certainty the many determinants of her display of femininity, but we could hypothesize that some of them might be related to her mother's possible attempts to rework old conflicts with her own mother by encouraging an idealized and dependent relationship with her daughter. Perhaps, too, despite her firmly held feminist views, Julia's mother was in part supportive of and pleased by Julia's display of a femininity that she could not allow herself to express. Julia could in this way be seen to be expressing a disowned characteristic of the mother. At the same time, father might be delighted by and very encouraging of his daughter's pretty femininity, not worried, inhibited, or discouraging as some fathers are about intimacy with such a flirtatious baby girl.

An important ingredient in this potent mix of influences is the degree of intensity vested in our toddler's relationship with each of his parents. He will have a unique relationship with each. One parent may be more absent or withdrawn and less available in the child's mind for identifications to take place, as well as less available in the other parent's mind as a buffer against over-involvement and mutual interdependency with the toddler.

Another important part of the development of a sense of core gender is your toddler's growing awareness of and investment in his body. His sense of his body as a source of pleasure and pride, coherent and integrated with boundaries in relation to others, has progressed. His confidence and trust in his body and what it can do as well as what it displays will also influence his feelings about himself as he tries to work out a sense of himself as a boy or girl.

Imaginative play

Play is the arena where experimentation with gender identity takes place. But as we have seen, play is important in many other respects. In particular, as the child gets older and has to moderate his aggressive urges in order to accommodate a more social world, play provides a space in which to act out aggressive feelings in a socially acceptable way. In chapter 4, Katy uses the toy wild animal to express her anger with her mother. Other toddlers will find all sorts of routes to express their more negative feelings, whether it is making the toy cars or the trains crash into each other or banging hard on musical instruments. They usually do it with great delight and gusto. Play is an outlet for these feelings, and it is important that children are encouraged to find constructive ways in which to channel these entirely understandable emotions. Aggression when rerouted through these different paths can become an important source of energy and achievement. Toddlers who experience their own hostile wishes as unacceptable risk becoming anxious, compliant, and placatory as they grow older, characteristics that will inhibit their development in many spheres, especially education.

The toddler's growing awareness of his own and others' minds

As the child moves towards his third birthday, imaginative play also becomes a place where he can learn about his own and others' minds. Very young children believe that their thoughts and others' thoughts accurately mirror the external world. They are unable to distinguish between fantasy and reality. Thoughts and feelings are therefore potentially very frightening to a young child. However, it is considered that, through pretend play with the participation of a benign adult, a young child begins to learn the distinction between thoughts, feelings, and fantasies about the self and the external world. As the adult and the child play together, the child learns to recognize that both he and the other adult are playing in an area of the mind where thoughts and feelings are representations of reality, not direct replicas of it, that they do not exactly mirror reality. The child develops the capacity to know that he knows that you know that what you are playing at is not real. Imaginative play then becomes safe, as well as being a shared experience. As with all these more mature abilities, however, there are frequent relapses to periods when there is a loss of that distinction.

It is helpful to know that even relatively old children (and sometimes adults) can lose the distinction between fantasy and reality. Some children, for example, continue to find clowns or Father Christmas or characters from films frightening because they seem so real and so like characters from their imaginary world. And if fantasy and reality are collapsed together in the shape of one of these characters, then other fantasies, such as murderous violent wishes, threaten also to come true in reality. The child's panic at such times is understandable. It may be that these fears emerge in terrifying nightmares, where the child cannot distinguish his dream from reality. Nightmares and bad dreams can occur in a toddler at a time of crisis or stress, where his real life experiences—perhaps of witnessing an accident or seeing a violent argument—have coincided with his destructive fantasies about, for example, people being hurt. Again it becomes hard for him not to believe that what he imagines will come true. At times like these, it can be helpful to talk over the scary experience and help him understand that he was not responsible for it, reminding him of the difference between the real and the imaginary worlds.

As children learn about others' minds they develop the ability to be empathic. You will remember how, in chapter 3, Julia was able to put herself in other children's shoes. She was able to speculate that Christopher might be crying because he had hurt himself and that Mary might be upset because she did not want to go home. As with Julia, in this chapter Sarah's ability to identify with and then reflect on other children's emotions makes it much easier for her to relate to them. As we can see in Sarah's afternoon vignette, her understanding of the predicament of the almost-a-baby newcomer who grabs the bowl allowed her to accept its loss, and her appreciation of Christopher's feelings about her grabbing the nozzle allowed her to drop the physical struggle and ask if she could have a turn. It becomes easier to play with other children when children can reflect and articulate others' emotions—they can share and take turns.

Learning about acceptable behaviour

With a growing awareness of others' minds and the beginnings of a capacity to empathize, the toddler begins to experience the early stages of a sense of guilt, and a sense of what is acceptable and unacceptable behaviour. The primary motivation for this, the precursor to a sense of conscience, is the fear of the loss of love of his parents. As we have seen, he wants to please his parents in order to gain their love, but all too often this wish conflicts with others that he wants gratified. A precondition for the toddler's moral development, then, is that he should feel loved and valued by his parents, and that he will feel the loss of their love if it is temporarily withdrawn because of some unacceptable behaviour. A child who has never felt loved will not notice its withdrawal and may not be able to distinguish between what is acceptable or unacceptable behaviour because he has never experienced the censure of those who love him.

At this stage, our toddler has no internal sense of guilt. He does not yet fully understand or remember why some behaviours meet with his parents' approval and others do not. He needs his parents or other friendly adults nearby to remind him. If they move away then, it is quite possible he will be tempted again to transgress. His internal sense of what is right and wrong only becomes firmly consolidated as he grows older. At this stage, when you say "No" he will not understand why the behaviour is wrong. Nor will he know necessarily that that behaviour is wrong when you are not there to witness it. He will only know that some of his behaviours lead to the loss of his parent's love and affection or that others seem to bring about an increase in their loving attention. He may test you time and time again to see your response to some of his behaviours, and it is important to try to be consistent because otherwise he will get mixed messages and may begin to think it is a bit of a game.

For you the parents, the older toddler brings an entirely new set of challenges. No longer required to be almost constantly available, you nevertheless have to be able to be in touch enough to be able to predict the times when your presence will be needed, even if from a bit more of a distance. Just as you thought you were through the worst of the tantrums, you find they reassert themselves and that the oppositional behaviour continues. For some parents, their child's new verbal skills are a source of a delight and a relief after witnessing his frustration at not being able to communicate easily. But for others, this can be wearing as the child makes his presence felt through endless chatter and questioning. Parents can sometimes feel quite pinned down by their child's verbal fluency. And, of course, their children may well be wanting to pin them down—after all, it is a very efficient way to gain their parents' attention.

Many parents find the question of how to deal with their child's unacceptable behaviour very difficult. As the children get older and bigger, it becomes much harder physically to lift them up out of or remove them from the problematic situation. By the time they are approaching 3 years, they can appear to behave quite naughtily and provocatively, and yet to express our disapproval may seem calculated and cruel. Some parents find it difficult to withdraw affection—won't it make their child feel unloved? Such parents can end up feeling so guilty they are unable to take control of the situation. Of course, it is possible for parents to be cruel to their children and to use extreme measures to let their child know they do not like what he is doing. However, usually, if your child values your love, it will only take a moment for him to know that it is threatened—that what he is doing is met with your displeasure. Momentarily you will have to indicate a lessening of love so that your child wants to regain it by changing what he is doing.

However, disciplining a child does not mean not loving him, even though momentarily he may feel unloved. Paradoxically it is, in fact, a sign of your love that you are strong enough to express your disapproval in this way. It will also probably help you and the child if disapproval is accompanied by conveying understanding that you know what he is feeling and how hard it is for him to give up his wishes to do what he wants in order to please you. In this way, he and you will keep in touch with your underlying feelings of concern for him. It will also help if you convey to him an increase in your pleasure when he does achieve what you want him to do. Parental guilt about imposing standards of behaviour on their toddler is sometimes a reflection of ambivalent feelings towards their child, which parents believe to be utterly unacceptable. A fear of imposing their will and the perception of such behaviour as abusive may, paradoxically, reflect an underlying resentment and hostility towards their child, which parents then have to protect their children from by being overindulgent. As a result, such toddlers can end up feeling anxious and uncomfortable with the power that they can exert over their parents, and the toddlers then become worried by their difficulties in regulating their emotions in situations of conflict.

The challenge for parents

A theme for this book has been the gradual process of separation between parents and toddler, and the growth of autonomy in parents and child alike. Some parents welcome this wholeheartedly at this stage, but others may be surprised by how sad they feel yet again to see their not-so-long-ago baby move into childhood with such alarming speed. Just as some parents feel acutely the loss of their child's dependent babyhood, others will feel acutely the loss of the companionship of their older toddler. Some parents who welcomed their child's move from the dependence of babyhood into the more accessible exploration and excitement of toddlerhood may know that they will miss their toddler's active, enquiring presence. As they become more able to cope with the outside world—to go to nursery school unaccompanied, say, or to play with friends without you there—they will of course be doing things, perhaps for the very first time, of which you will be entirely unaware. They will encounter people you may have never met and may play games you never see. You have kept such a close watch over them for the first three years that such relinquishment of control and involvement over their daily activities may be hard indeed to tolerate. The temptation to keep them attached and protected from the outside world can be very strong and can make it hard for parents to contemplate the next step.

Such feelings are entirely natural. Just like our toddlers, we too can be stressed by times of transition. But unlike our toddlers, we also know that to respond to transitions by withdrawing from the toddlers' demands will inhibit our lives and deprive them of the vitality that comes from facing the challenges of the unknown. A fulfilled adult life requires the capacity to have autonomy but also to be able to be intimate and dependent. At this stage, we have to demonstrate to our children our capacity to tolerate this tension by letting them go. True love allows for freedom as well as intimacy.

suggested reading

In writing this I have drawn on reading and experience in psychoanalysis and child development gained over many years. I am indebted to many scholars in the field, and it would be impossible to acknowledge them all here. However, the following is a short list of some of sources that may be of interest to parents who would like to explore a topic further or to think about their child's future development.

Dilys Daws. *Through the Night: Helping Parents and Sleepless Infants.* London: Free Association Books, 1989.

Selma Fraiberg. *The Magic Years: Understanding and Handling the Problems of Early Childhood.* New York: Scribner's, 1959.

Peter Hobson. *The Cradle of Thought: Exploring the Origins of Thinking.* London: Macmillan, 2002.

Alicia Lieberman. *The Emotional Life of the Toddler.* New York: Free Press, 1993.

Linda C. Mayes & Donald J. Cohen. *The Yale Child Study Center Guide to Understanding Your Child: Healthy Development from Birth to Adolescence.* Boston: Little Brown, 2002.

For readers interested in deepening their understanding of some of the psychoanalytic ideas in the book or their technical knowledge of child development, the following sources may be of interest:

Sigmund Freud (1920). *Beyond the Pleasure Principle.* In: *The Standard Edition of the Complete Psychological Works of Sigmund Freud, Vol. 18* (pp. 4–67). London: Hogarth Press, 1955.

Eric Rayner, Angela Joyce, James Rose, Mary Twyman, & Christopher Clulow. *Human Development: An Introduction to the Psychodynamics of Human Growth and Aging* (4th edition). New York: Brunner-Routledge, 2005.

Allan N. Schore. *Affect Regulation and the Origins of the Self.* Hillsdale, NJ: Lawrence Erlbaum Associates, 1994.

Daniel N. Stern. *The Interpersonal World of the Infant.* New York: Basic Books, 1985.

D. W. Winnicott. *Playing and Reality.* New York: Basic Books, 1971.

index